The HumanMagnet Syndrome
Why We Love People Who Hurt Us

Ross Rosenberg M.Ed., LCPC, CADC

www.pesi.com

PESI Publishing & Media

"Ross Rosenberg's important work, 'The Human Magnet Syndrome: Why We Love People Who Hurt Us,' challenges us to continue looking at relationship dynamics to see how our experiences affected us and will continue to affect others. Join this forward-looking movement by reading a book that draws on the discoveries of the past, but adds more wisdom combined with effective answers. It's both the next step in evolution and a revelation.

I recommend 'The Human Magnet Syndrome' to those who work in social services, education, chemical dependency or the counseling fields and to the people they touch. It's time to wake up and this brilliant book sounds the alarm we need."

- Melody Beattie, author of 18 books, including best-selling
Codependent No More and Language of Letting Go

"Born in the cauldron of personal experience of suffering and healing, and honed through years of professional experience, this book will help anyone understand the attractors of love and consequent suffering. I recommend it to couples who are mystified by the depth and repetition of their pain and joy, and to therapists whose destiny is to help them."

- Harville Hendrix, Ph.D., National Couples Counseling expert,
speaker, and co-author with Helen LaKelly Hunt of *Making Marriage Simple:*
Transform the Relationship You Have into the Relationship You Want

"Rosenberg offers a much needed, accessible explanation about how love, sex and relationships can go awry — and what each of us can do to become more empowered and engaged in our lifelong process of building community and family."

- Robert Weiss, LCSW, CSAT-S, author,
psychotherapist, educator, sex and relationship disorders expert

"Refreshingly intuitive and innovative, Rosenberg unravels the mystery of self-sabotaging relationship patterns. A must read."

- Randi Kreger, coauthor of best-selling *Stop Walking on Eggshells*
and 3 other books on Borderline and Narcissistic Personality Disorders, host of the
on-line forum "Welcome to Oz" (www.BPDCentral.com), and *Psychology Today* blogger

"Many couples have a give and take relationship. The takers will not read this book. The givers need to. For those who give too much, there is freedom in these pages. Clarity begins here. Learn why you are constantly frustrated no matter how much you give to your partner. Get this book and give yourself a gift."

- Peter Pearson, Ph.D., co-founder of The Couples Institute

ABOUT THE AUTHOR

Ross A. Rosenberg, M.Ed., LCPC, CADC, is an expert in the field of dysfunctional relationships, codependency and sex, love and Internet addictions, for which he provides comprehensive psychotherapy, training and consultation services. He is the owner of Clinical Care Consultants, a counseling center in the northern suburbs of Chicago. Since 1988, Ross has been an administrator, professional trainer and psychotherapist.

Ross's first book, *The Human Magnet Syndrome: Why We Love People Who Hurt Us*. draws on his 25 years of experience in the mental health, social service and/or child welfare fields. He also is a leading national seminar speaker and expert psychotherapist. By the end of 2013, Ross will have presented his current seminar, "Emotional Manipulators & Codependents: Understanding the Attraction" in 27 states. Ross is currently writing a follow-up book, which will be a guide for codependents who desire to be in healthy relationships.

Ross's psychotherapy services enable his clients to achieve balance, inner peace and feelings of personal efficacy. He believes that, "within a warm and respectful therapeutic relationship lies the power to overcome seemingly overwhelming obstacles."

www.HumanMagnetSyndrome.com
www.RossRosenbergTherapy.com
www.ClinicalCareConsultants.com

DEDICATION

This book is dedicated to my wife, Korrel Rosenberg, the partner of my dreams: a collaborator in life and my best friend. It is because of our shared patience with each other and our never-ending optimism for our future, we both can say we finally got it right. I am truly blessed to have a wonderfully loving, supportive and understanding partner who believes in me as much as I do in her.

The book is also dedicated to my son, Benjamin Rosenberg, who has inspired me with a sense of purpose to be the type of father that I could be proud of. Ben's confident and calm resolve to be his own person has convinced me that dysfunctional family generational patterns do not necessarily have to move forward.

I additionally dedicated this book to my deceased mother, Mikki Rosenberg. Her spirit of unconditional love and compassion forever lives in my heart and has imbued every page of this book.

Lastly, this book is dedicated to all of the courageous readers who are seeking true and healthy love, but need to first overcome their own painful and challenging psychological obstacles.

Copyright © 2013 by Ross A. Rosenberg, M.Ed., LCPC, CADC
Published by
PESI Publishing & Media
3839 White Avenue
Eau Claire, WI 54702

Printed in the United States of America
Cover Design: Matt Pabich
Layout Design: Amy Rubenzer
Edited by: Marietta Whittlesey & Kayla Omtvedt

Library of Congress Cataloging-in-Publication Data

Rosenberg, Ross A.

  The human magnet syndrome : Why we love people who hurt us /
by Ross A. Rosenberg, M.Ed., LCPC, CADC.

    pages cm

  ISBN-13: 978-1-936128-31-0 (pbk.)

  ISBN-10: 1-936128-31-4 (pbk.)

  1. Codependency. 2. Codependents--Rehabilitation. 3. Emotional
conditioning. I. Title. II. Title: Why we love people who hurt us.

  RC569.5.C63R67 2013

  616.85'81--dc23

                              2013004163

www.pesi.com
PESI Publishing & Media

TABLE OF CONTENTS

PREFACE

How have I gotten this far? Why after so many failed relationships did I finally meet a woman with whom I could share a stable, emotionally-intimate and mutually-loving relationship? To write this book, I knew I had to answer these seemingly impossible questions. I needed to reconcile why, at age 45, after so many failed relationships, I was finally able to experience a healthy long-term romantic relationship.[1] Although it has been a long and emotionally exhausting journey for me, I am glad I never gave up on the ideal that one day I would find that one very special person with whom I could share healthy "true love."

The hypotheses and theories included in this book have been marinating in my mind for well over two decades. It wasn't that long ago (November of 2010) when I told Korrel, my lovely wife, I was ready to write a book about dysfunctional relationships. Korrel naturally asked me for the details of my grand pronouncement. All I could say was "it is in my head and it's a perfect set of ideas." I went on to explain that it would represent elements of my whole life and career and had been occupying space in my mind for over 20 years. With an incredulous and confused look, she said, "Really, a book in your head for that long...how does that work?" I continued to confuse her with my next statement: "The book will write itself...all I need to do is get myself in front of a computer and put my hands on a keyboard." Korrel's next response warmed my heart: She smiled at me and told me how much she believed in me and that anything I write would indeed be perfect.

It was true, once my fingers touched the keyboard, the words leapt onto the screen. As I typed, I was accessing a whole personal library of memories, thoughts and ideas. From my fingertips came forth a set of persuasive and illustrative explanations for dysfunctional romantic attraction (relationships). One chapter at a time the book took shape. While writing the book, I often wondered from where all these ideas had come.

---

[1] When I met Korrel Crawford, who became my wife in December of 2008, I was 47.

At times it seemed like I was both the writer and the appreciative reader, separated only by my hands on the keyboard.

Looking back, it is clear now, that this book has been "aging" in my mind, like a great bottle of wine. It developed into an exposition about a magnetic-like force that compels opposite personality types to be unconsciously and unwittingly drawn together into an enduring but miserable dysfunctional romantic relationship. The book attempts to make sense of the phenomenon that compels so many of us to become romantically involved with harmful and narcissistic romantic partners, who would, in some manner, be oddly reminiscent of one of our parents. My book also explains why so many of us remain in dysfunctional and toxic relationships – with partners who would always hurt us, rarely care for us, and always be the person we believed we loved.

This book draws from my own struggles with dysfunctional romantic relationships. I write about why we romantic hopefuls would fall in love with someone who, in the beginning, seemed virtually perfect; who, in an instant, would become our lover, best friend, and confidant – our soul mate. Our seemingly perfect mate would share our titillating excitement of physical attraction and join us in a roller coaster ride of emotional and romantic euphoria. With our supposed "true love" we would instantly experience overpowering urges to merge emotionally, physically and sexually. Our bodies would reel from powerful and hypnotic sensations; our minds would race wildly with excitement and anticipation. We would be convinced that we were perfectly matched partners – twin flames of one romantic hearth.

What felt so right, so perfect, would remain that way for no longer than a few months. Despite the rapturous beginning of our supposed soul-mate experience, the relationship would inevitably crash and burn. The hot flames of passion would predictably transform into frustration, impatience, resentment and regret. Our fantasy lover, before our very eyes, would morph into an angry, controlling, narcissistic person who would hurt us while all the time insisting she or he loved us. We would be left feeling powerless to set safe boundaries or to break up. In each case, we would feel alone, unloved and, ultimately, resentful.

Looking back, the pattern should have been crystal clear: I would continue to ride the merry-go-round of dysfunctional relationships until I figured out why I kept making the same relationship mistakes over and over again. Being a psychotherapist didn't seem to make finding these answers any easier. I will never forget when, eight years ago, a good friend gave me life-changing feedback about my dysfunctional relationship patterns. She told me that every woman I had fallen in love with "was really the same person but with a different face." She warned me that if I didn't figure out the underlying reason for my dysfunctional relationship choices, I would be stuck in a never ending cycle of love and disappointment. This very wise and insightful friend was able to see in me what I was blind to. This simple comment shook my emotional foundation. For the first time, I considered that maybe it wasn't bad luck after all, but perhaps, there was something about me that had contributed to my relationship failures.

Through my friend's wise counsel I was able to realize that until I resolved my own core psychological issues, I was destined to perpetually repeat my relationship failures. I began to comprehend that deeply entrenched and unconscious forces within me compelled me to repeat my childhood trauma of feeling alone, unimportant and emotionally lost. As a direct result of this discovery, I committed myself to a psychological journey of discovery, healing and transformation. I made a promise to myself that I would not stop this journey until I could actualize my dreams for true and healthy love. It has been a difficult path though. Breaking a cycle that was embedded in the deepest recesses of my psyche would take time, effort and an unwavering belief in an ideal.

Narcotics Anonymous is credited with saying, "Insanity is doing the same thing over and over again and expecting different results." He must have understood my rollercoaster experience with romantic partners. Why was I continuing with my dysfunctional relationship follies if I knew something was wrong? Was this my own form of insanity? At the time, I thought so. There came a time in my life when I was ready to reach way down deep, embrace my deepest fears, seize control of my future, and finally stop the insanity in my life. To fulfill my promise to myself, my first move was to figure out why I was habitually attracted to women who, despite my attentiveness and generosity, would harm me. I knew I had to first dig deep into the convoluted fabric of my emotional past.

Sunday, November 20, 2005, was the day when I hit my emotional bottom. On that day, I attended Oakton Community College's (in Des Plaines, Illinois) Men's Day – an event that promoted exploration, discussion and self-evaluation of male issues. Out of approximately 400 registrants, there were about 20 women. It wasn't a coincidence that on that day, a beautiful woman and I latched onto one another in a mix of compelling dialogue and flirtation. The pulsating adrenalin and dopamine rush brought me once again to the brink of yet another dysfunctional romantic relationship. This time was different: I recognized the relationship disaster before it unfolded. In a discernible moment, I made a decision to stop my personal insanity! I refused to let myself fall into yet another relationship death spiral. This time I was resolute: I was going to vanquish the demons of my past and blaze a path toward true and healthy love.

I had simply reached my emotional bottom. I was ready to stop participating in my own personal nightmare, ready to put an end to my turnstile-like dysfunctional relationship patterns. I was prepared to embrace my "insanity" and to work myself out of my self-defeating relationship patterns. Thanks to this lovely woman, I made a resolution to make wholesale changes in my life. I promised myself to fight the demons of my youth that compelled me to reenact my childhood condition of loneliness and sorrow. I had finally become courageous enough to acknowledge the unbearable grief and shame of decades of failed relationships. I was ready and willing to do whatever personal and emotional work was necessary. I was determined to fall in love with a woman who would love and respect me as much as I did her – a woman, who instead of hurting me, would affirm and nurture me. Thus began my personal recovery and the foundation of understanding that ultimately would become the impetus for this book.

**"If I am not for myself,
who will be for me?
But if I am only for myself,
who am I?
If not now, when?"**

Rabbi Hillel (30 BC - 10 AD)

INTRODUCTION

The book is about love and the pursuit of one's life-long romantic partner. Since the dawn of modern civilization, men and women have been magnetically and irresistibly drawn together into romantic relationships, not so much by what they see, feel and think, but more by invisible forces. When individuals with healthy emotional backgrounds meet, the irresistible "love force" creates a sustainable, reciprocal and stable relationship. Codependents and emotional manipulators are similarly enveloped in a seductive dreamlike state; however, it will later unfold into a painful "seesaw" of love, pain, hope and disappointment. The soul mate of the codependent's dreams will become the emotional manipulator of their nightmares.

About 30 years ago, my dad joked (or I thought was a joke): "The *soul mate* of your dreams is gonna become the *cellmate* of your nightmares." It takes some of us decades to realize that our parents were actually a lot smarter than we gave them credit for. What I thought was just a flippant and cynical comment would later help to define my understanding of dysfunctional romantic relationships. I would never have guessed that my dad's off-the-cuff remark would contain so much psychological merit. Perhaps he understood that the initial wondrous feelings of joy and euphoria would never last. It would inevitably transform into something more insidiously harmful, and the sweetheart of our dreams would end up as a "ball and chain" locked around our ankle for the rest of our lives.

For those of us raised by psychologically healthy parents, who were unconditionally loving and affirming, the wondrous "love at first sight" story might have actually happened to you. If so, you would be one of those fortunate individuals who, for the rest of your life, could boast about your remarkable love at first sight moment and how perfect it was and has been. However, if you were raised by abusive, neglectful or absent parents, it is likely that you experienced the blissful love at first sight experience, but it was likely short-lived and highly disappointing.

Predictably, but not surprisingly, the "perfect" lover will transform into someone that may be unrecognizable. Within a few months, perhaps even weeks, their attractive, alluring traits will be replaced by a selfish and self-centered demeanor, which will take center stage in the new relationship and you will feel powerless to stop him or her.

A person, whose parents deprived them of unconditional love during their childhood, especially the first five to six years, will likely be drawn to a narcissistic romantic partner by a magnet-like force from which it will seem impossible to break free. This magnetic force, or the Human Magnet Syndrome, has the raw power to bring codependents and narcissists together in a perfect storm of love and dysfunction. The magnetic power of this dysfunctional love will keep these seemingly opposite lovers together despite their shared misery and eager hopes of changing each other. The dream of perfect and everlasting love will sadly never come to fruition. The soul mate dream will inevitably morph into the cellmate reality.

When it comes to romantic relationships, we all are indeed human magnets! I chose the title of this book, "The Human Magnet Syndrome," because it succinctly captures the attraction dynamic of dysfunctional love. All of us are compelled to fall in love with a specific personality type that is dichotomously opposite from our own. Like metal magnets, human magnets are attracted to each other when their opposite personalities or "magnetic roles" are perfectly matched. The bond created by perfectly matched "human magnets" is interminably powerful, binding two lovers together despite consequences or shared unhappiness. In a codependent and emotional manipulator[2] relationship, this magnetic force will likely create a long-term dysfunctional relationship. Conversely, with healthy romantic partners, the Human Magnet Syndrome results in relationships that are empowering, affirming and mutually-satisfying.

My life experience, which includes 25 years as a psychotherapist, addiction specialist, consultant, professional trainer and business owner, has taught me that we are all "human magnets," who are irresistibly attracted to a romantic partner whose personality or "magnetic charge" is perfectly opposite, exquisitely compatible, and equally as powerful as our own. I coined the term "The Human Magnet Syndrome" to help others understand the ever-present relationship force that inexorably brings dysfunctional lovers together, while rendering them powerless to break free from each other.

I developed the Continuum of Self Theory to illustrate, describe and even quantify the ever-present attraction that compels opposite personality types, such as codependents and emotional manipulators, to come together in a lasting but dysfunctional romantic relationship. The reader will learn that

---

[2] The exact nature of these disorders/conditions will be explained in subsequent chapters.

all potential romantic partners, healthy or dysfunctional, are "magnetically" attracted to each other and are emotionally compatible as a direct result of their perfectly matched opposite self-orientations (personalities). This theory accounts for the full range of relationship possibilities – from healthy to dysfunctional. Through an explanation and application of the continuum of self theory, the reader will learn about the ubiquitous and omnipresent "love force" that affects each and every person who desires to find the romantic partner of their dreams.

On the continuum of self, codependency and emotional manipulation disorders are dichotomously opposite personality types. I suggest that we all fit somewhere on the continuum of self. This continuum measures a specific personality trait – a self-orientation. A self-orientation is defined as the manner in which we love, care for and respect ourselves and others while in a relationship. If we have an "others" self-orientation, we are more concerned with the needs of others, while placing less importance on having our own needs fulfilled. If we have a "self" self-orientation, we tend to be more preoccupied with our own needs, while ignoring the wants and desires of our loved ones.

This book was inspired by my own journey to overcome the forces that invisibly influenced my own dysfunctional relationship choices. The concepts and ideas that define this book were inspired by my attempts to discover why, as a former therapist once told me, my "relationship picker" was so badly broken. Since I never intended to be unhappy in my relationships, and greatly suffered as a result of them, I needed to identify and isolate the reasons behind my dysfunctional relationship patterns in order to change them once and for all.

Through a great deal of challenging and difficult personal work, I eventually figured out why I habitually gravitated toward harmful romantic partners. I realized that my adult relationship patterns were distinctly impacted by the manner in which my narcissistic father and codependent mother had raised me.[3] Through this work, I connected this same developmental process to all children who were brought up by a narcissistic or emotional manipulator parent. I also learned that adult relationship patterns, healthy or dysfunctional, are always impacted by the type of parenting a child receives during the first five or six years of life, their formative years. With these insights, I was better able to provide psychotherapy that would facilitate fundamental personality change. I have helped my codependent clientele reconcile and heal their childhood trauma that I refer to as *"the original condition."* The original condition is the trauma and/or damaging circumstance that is foundationally responsible for dysfunctional adult relationship patterns.

[3] I have come to understand my parents' shortcomings and have forgiven them. They, too, were victims of challenging childhoods.

The reader will come to understand why the human desire to be understood and to love and be loved compels us to find a romantic companion. A human "love drive" motivates us to seek a companion who we hope will understand our struggles, validate our pain, affirm our dreams and, most of all, co-create an explosion of emotional and sexual excitement. We can't help it; we are naturally inclined to look for someone who will spark our deepest desires and who will join with us on a rollercoaster ride of sexual and emotional excitement and romance.

The book will explain why patient, giving and selfless individuals – codependents - are predictably attracted to selfish, self-centered and controlling partners – emotionally manipulators. Like clockwork, codependents and emotional manipulators find themselves habitually and irresistibly drawn into a relationship that begins with emotional and sexual highs, but later transforms into a painful and disappointing dysfunctional "relationship dance." The dance of the codependent and emotional manipulator is paradoxical in nature in that the two opposite personalities participate in a relationship that begins with excitement, joy and euphoria, but always transforms into one that is strewn with drama, conflict and feelings of being trapped.

This book is about real-life relationships – common everyday relationships – that many of us have experienced, *but wish we hadn't.* It is also about codependents and emotional manipulators and the ubiquitous "magnetic force" that brings them together into a lasting dysfunctional romantic relationship. The reader will learn why codependents and emotional manipulators are always attracted to each other and why, despite major personal and emotional upheavals, they remain together.

This book has the capacity to change lives. It examines the intricacies of the dysfunctional relationship dynamic shared between codependents and emotional manipulators. This dynamic will be illustrated through my continuum of self model, which ties together the complex web of underlying psychological forces that "magnetizes" emotional manipulators and codependents into enduring and mutually unavoidable relationships. This book will explain the nature of these binding relationships which are typically immune to personal or professional assistance.

In this book, I write about concepts, explanations and paradigms that represent the plight of the person who was raised by an emotional manipulator. The development of these concepts and theories has been distinctly influenced by my efforts to be a both a psychologically healthier person and a more effective psychotherapist. Concepts like "The Golden Rules of The Helping Professions," "The Dance," "The Continuum of Self Theory" and "The Human Magnet Syndrome" were all derived from the sum total of my life experiences. This book comes from the deepest recesses of my mind, my heart and my soul. It is the living and breathing representation of all the experiences that have molded me – both personally and professionally. With gratitude, I acknowledge the many brilliant and talented individuals from whom I have learned, grown and benefited; indeed, I am standing on the shoulders of giants. I also want to acknowledge the profound impact that my psychotherapy clients have had on my professional growth. The voices of these clients are reflected in every page of this book. I am truly grateful.

If this book had just one purpose, it would be to give hope to others who, like myself, yearned for "true love" but, instead, kept finding "true dysfunction." I am hopeful that the continuum of self theory, as well as the other conceptual material in this book, will help the reader to understand why so many of us fall prey to our dysfunctional instincts. It is my hope that helping professionals, as well as the general public, will benefit from this book. I have gone to great lengths to reduce complicated relationship dynamics into intuitive, concrete and relatable explanations. Mental health professionals and general audiences alike should learn what specifically drives and sustains the emotional manipulator and codependent relationship.

The more accessible and practical a book is, the more it may alter the course of the lives of those who read it. I believe that straight-forward and simple explanations for human behavior are often more useful than those that are multileveled, complicated and unintentionally convoluted. Of course, there are many elements of the human psyche that cannot and should not be reduced or simplified. But why can't we have a blueprint for the attraction process that everyone can understand? Why make something complicated when it doesn't have to be? There is no rule that an advanced degree, certification or special training is needed to understand psychological phenomenon. Sometimes difficult situations, such as dysfunctional relationship patterns, can be understood through simple explanations. It is my hope that this book will provide readers with an accessible, practical and clear understanding of dysfunctional relationship patterns.

The concepts included in this book should have a familiar "ring" to most readers, as they describe a universal human experience. These concepts (explanations) have already helped hundreds of my clients, and thousands of seminar participants – all of whom sought information about destructive dysfunctional relationship patterns. I hope this book becomes an essential resource to those individuals who crave emotional freedom from their traumatic and emotionally burdensome pasts, as well as to clinicians who treat these clients.

This book is also written for the courageous and determined souls who, through a healing and transformative psychotherapy process, may be able to finally experience true and healthy love. Perhaps my greatest ambition for the book is that it may inspire readers to extricate themselves from their own destructive relationships, while also motivating them to develop a capacity to find and sustain a healthy and mutually satisfying loving romantic relationship. Some readers may learn that they also have a broken "relationship picker," which would explain why they consistently participate in unhealthy or dysfunctional long-term relationships. Readers are likely to reach a deeper understanding of the emotional manipulation disorders, codependency and the magnetic-like relationship dynamic between the two.

I hope this book instills optimism and a sense of hope into those individuals who are ready to take a courageous leap and commence a deeply personal and emotional journey to find healthy long-term romantic relationships. I know from first-hand experience that this is both possible and well worth the work. Like my psychotherapy clients, I have resolved to stop suffering at the hands of my own unconscious mind. Over the last 15 years, I have dug deep and fought hard to learn about the pervasive forces that kept drawing me into relationships that resulted in self-destruction, emotional pain and suffering. As a result of my unshakable promise to myself to break my own pattern of "magnetic" attraction to emotional manipulators, I would eventually meet my lovely and beautiful wife, Korrel. Freeing myself from what seemed like a relationship curse has made an indescribably positive impact on my life.

Shouldn't we all choose to look honestly and courageously into ourselves and seek to understand our deeper, unconscious motives? Shouldn't we also strive to heal deeply imbedded psychological wounds that without resolution will likely block us from ever finding our soul mate of our dreams? The answer is a resounding yes! Without courage and the resolute willpower to change our relational path, we will needlessly suffer the plight of unrealized goals, aspirations and dreams.

Lastly, I hope this book inspires and instructs mental health practitioners who desire to lead their clients in the direction of healthy, affirming and mutually romantic love. With a more complete understanding of codependency and the emotional manipulation disorders, mental health practitioners should have greater opportunities to help their adult clients to overcome their destructive and dysfunctional relationship patterns.

At the end of the day, I am a therapist who is emotionally invested in the lives of his clients. I have always believed that I have the best job in the world. I still can't believe I get paid for making people happy and helping them actualize their ambitions and dreams! The following prose speaks to my desire to help my clients find their "oasis" of freedom and hope.

If hope and happiness always seem a tomorrow away,
If too many days end in sadness and a lack of fulfillment,
If your heart and your mind speak different languages,
If love of self and others seems to be beyond your grasp,
If you live in a desert of sadness and loneliness,
but seek an oasis of freedom and hope, I can help.

– Ross Rosenberg

Chapter 1

The Inevitability of Our Future

As much as we would like to, we cannot avoid certain indisputable facts of life: We will have to pay taxes, we will get older, we will most likely gain a few pounds, and we will always be connected to our childhood. Sigmund Freud was right, we are, indeed, creatures of our past; affected more by our formative years (first five to six years of life) than by recent events and circumstances. Although genes play a significant role in determining our adult selves, the manner in which we were cared for as a child is integrally connected to our adult mental health. Whether we embrace our unique childhood history, or if we try to mute, forget or even deny it, there is no way of denying its impact on our lives.

The experiential landscape of our childhood directly impacts our future adult relationships. Specifically, the manner in which we were parented during our formative years is directly connected to the quality of our adult relationships. If you were fortunate, you may have had a childhood that was absent of major trauma, abuse, deprivation or neglect. As one of the fortunate ones, you would have had parents who made mistakes, but who also unconditionally loved and cared for you. Just by being yourself, despite your imperfections, you would have proved to your parents that all babies are perfect and the gift of life is sacred. Your healthy but not perfect parents would have been intrinsically motivated to foster your personal and emotional growth, not because they had to, but because they believed you deserved it! The only requirement to receive your parents' love and nurturing was to just be your genuine self – just to be. Consequently, you would have become a part of a multigenerational pattern of emotionally healthy children; you would have become a balanced and emotionally healthy adult. If you decided to have children, you would perpetuate the positive parenting "karma" by raising your own emotionally healthy child.

The child of psychologically unhealthy parents would also participate in a similar multigenerational pattern; just one that is perpetually dysfunctional. If one of your parents was an emotional manipulator, you would have been born to this world with expectations that if achieved, would motivate your narcissistic parent to love and nurture you. Provided you were able to maintain your parents' fantasy about what you should be like, you would likely receive their conditional love and conditional attention. By maintaining your parents' fantasies for parenthood, you would be their proud accomplishment – a trophy of sorts. As a direct result of your ability to accommodate your parents' narcissistic needs, as an adult you would develop codependency traits or would become a codependent. As an adult you would instinctively be attracted to a lover who would unconsciously remind you of your narcissistic parent – an emotional manipulator.

However, if you were unable to be your parents' "trophy child," you would trigger their own feelings of shame, anger and insecurity, which they would project onto you. As a child who is unable to make their narcissistic parent feel good about her or himself, you would likely be subjected to deprivation, neglect and/or abuse. Relaxing and enjoying the wonders of childhood would never be yours. Your lonely, deprived, and/or abusive childhood would lay the foundation for your future poor mental health and the consequent development of one of the emotional manipulator disorders. As an adult, just like your own parents, you would automatically and instinctively be attracted to romantic partners who would accept or tolerate your narcissism.

All parents, whether they are psychologically healthy or unhealthy, provide their children with experiences and memories that will ultimately result in an automatic relationship guide for their adult relationships. Children simply soak up their parents' treatment of them. If they are blessed, they might be the lucky recipients of a relationship GPS of sorts that will consistently guide them to the right place, right time and right person – all the time. The not- so-fortunate child may inherit a broken relationship manual, which will likely lead them astray in their pursuit of loving, safe and happy relationships. Although the broken guide may seem permanent, the human spirit has remarkable transformative potential. Because humans are capable of healing and transforming, as well as rising above the seemingly indisputable forces of our childhood, we do not have to be the torch-bearers of our parents' life sentence. We are all imbued with the capability to grow and learn from our mistakes. Many of us, with hard work, can get a chance to overturn what once seemed like a life sentence of future dysfunctional relationships.

CHAPTER 2
Codependents, Emotional Manipulators and Their "Dance"

Psychotherapists often rely on analogies and metaphors to assist their clients with complicated and painful emotional concepts. The therapeutic use of an analogy connects people to specific feelings and thoughts that otherwise would be inaccessible. As a clinician and a writer, I am often compelled to drive home a point by telling a story, making a comparison, or using creative figures of speech. For this book especially, I use analogies and metaphors to facilitate a deeper intellectual understanding and emotional connection to my concepts and explanations. Using them reduces complex ideas into relatable explanations, taking difficult-to-comprehend intellectual concepts and communicating them more effectively.

The Healing Power of Analogies and Metaphors

The use of an analogy or metaphor is especially helpful when working with trauma victims – such as adults who were raised by a neglectful and/or abusive emotional manipulator. A well-placed analogy or metaphor can facilitate an unrealized emotional connection or intellectual understanding of an anxiety- provoking memory which may have been previously blocked from the client's awareness. There is nothing more rewarding than when a well-placed analogy or metaphor creates a breakthrough moment. When it is spot-on, the resulting "light bulb" reaction or "aha moment" is priceless. I believe I speak for most psychotherapists when I say that we live for moments when everything "clicks" and our client arrives at an understanding that, until that moment, had eluded him. It has always been extraordinarily rewarding when I bring a codependent client to an "aha moment" when, because of a well-timed metaphor, they are able to connect to a deeper understanding of their problems, especially their dysfunctional relationship patterns.

Of all of the metaphors I use in psychotherapy, the "dance" has had the most positively powerful therapeutic effect on my clients, especially the codependents. The dance metaphor aptly and succinctly communicates the psychological dynamics of a codependent-narcissistic romantic relationship. Moreover, it simply illustrates the powerlessness codependents experience when in a relationship with a narcissistic romantic partner. My dance metaphor and later the essay have helped my psychotherapy clients to better and more deeply understand their dysfunctional relationship patterns. By simplistically reducing a person's predilection to choose "dance partners" who are irresistibly attractive, but harmfully controlling, the therapy shifts into a higher gear (another metaphor!).

According to the dictionary, a dance is defined as "rhythmical and sequential steps, gestures, or bodily motions that match the speed and rhythm of a piece of music." My definition for a "relationship dance" metaphor is virtually the same: "rhythmical and sequential steps, gestures, and romantic behaviors that match the speed and rhythm of each dance partner's personality and relationship expectation." Codependents and emotional manipulators participate in a dance-like phenomenon that ultimately creates a lasting dysfunctional relationship or "dancing partnership." "Dance partners" with oppositely matched dysfunctional personalities often participate in a dramatic, rollercoaster-like pathological relationship that continues despite one side's unhappiness or desire for the "dance" to stop.

Let's talk about the dancing. As with any successful dancing partnership, each partner is experienced, familiar, and acutely attuned to their partner's dance style and their idiosyncratic dance moves. To be successful on the dance floor, the two partners need to be compatible or work well together. The codependent and emotional manipulator succeed on the dance floor because of their complementary and well-matched dysfunctional personalities or "dance styles." The balancing of personality types, "dancing styles," ties these individuals together in a perpetual dance partnership, even if one or both partners are unhappy with the partnership. The well-matched dysfunctional dancers perform magnificently on the dance floor, because they are able instinctively to predict each other's moves. It is as if they have always danced together. To onlookers, this couple dances fluidly and gracefully, seeming like they have been perfecting their dance moves their whole lives. Each dancer knows their role: The emotional manipulator always leads and controls the "dance" while the codependent follows and acquiesces. Dysfunctional compatibility is the driving force behind this dynamic dancing duo.

As perfectly compatible dancing partners, the emotional manipulator dancer is the "yin" to the codependent's "yang." The narcissistic traits of an emotional manipulator make them an attractive choice to a codependent, who is typically comfortable in the role of giving, sacrificing, and being passive. Codependents are naturally drawn to emotional manipulators, because they feel comfortable and familiar with a person who knows how to direct, control and lead. The codependent's dancing skills are distinctly connected to their reflexive dysfunctional agility – to be attuned to the cues, gestures and self-serving movements of their emotional manipulator partner. Codependents expertly and adeptly predict and anticipate their emotional manipulator partner's each and every step, while experiencing the dance as a positive but passive experience.

Conversely, emotional manipulator "dancers" are drawn to codependent partners because they are allowed to feel strong, secure, in control and dominant in an activity that brings them much attention, praise, and love. They habitually choose codependent "dance" partners because with them they are allowed to maintain the center focus, lead the direction of the dance, and ultimately determine where, when and how the dance will proceed.

Like a good bottle of wine, my understanding of the dysfunctional dance partnership matured and developed over time into an idea that was palatable and appreciated by a larger audience. My dance metaphor seemed to consistently help my codependent clients achieve more insight and a deeper understanding of their habitual and dysfunctional relationship patterns with their narcissistic partners. The dance explanation was, at the surface level, a simple way to explain the complicated conscious and unconscious process that compelled them to experience prospective narcissistic romantic partners as alluring, attractive and intensely desirable.

The dance explanation was helpful to my codependent clients in two ways. Most obviously, it helped them understand their persistent dysfunctional attraction pattern to hurtful and selfish romantic partners. Secondly, it helped them to break their pattern of always "dancing" with a person who initially felt so right but ultimately would reveal themselves to be so wrong for them. With a deeper understanding of their dysfunctional patterns, over time my codependent clients would develop the insight, personal power and confidence to break free from their dysfunctional relationship patterns. Released from their propensity to fall in love with emotional manipulators, these "recovering" codependents would finally be able, and very motivated, to fall into the arms of a loving, attractive, and emotionally healthy dance partner.

In 2007, following an inspiring breakthrough therapy session, I wrote my essay, "Codependency, Don't Dance!" It was an immediate hit with my codependent clients. The essay seemed to galvanize their understanding of their dysfunctional and self-defeating relationship choices. Since writing the essay, it has become the most requested piece of my written work. Over the past five years, since it was written, the essay has helped hundreds of clients to analyze, and ultimately understand, their seemingly mysterious and habitual relationship patterns with emotional manipulators. The dance concept works, because it is a universally understood metaphor that crosses the divide of culture, gender, age and sexual orientation. It connects us to an essential and elemental human desire to seek romantic partners who complement our expectations, experience and perspective on what is normal and acceptable.

Codependency, Don't Dance!

The inherently dysfunctional "codependency dance" requires two opposite but distinctly balanced partners: the pleaser/fixer (codependent) and the taker/controller (narcissist/addict). Codependents, who are giving, sacrificing, and consumed with the needs and desires of others, do not know how to emotionally disconnect or avoid romantic relationships with individuals who are narcissistic – individuals who are selfish, self-centered, controlling, and harmful to them. Codependents habitually find themselves on a "dance floor" attracted to partners who are a perfect counter-match to their uniquely passive, submissive and acquiescent dance style.

As natural followers in their relationship "dance," codependents are passive and accommodating dance partners. Codependents find narcissistic dance partners deeply appealing as they are perpetually attracted to their charm, boldness, confidence and domineering personality. When codependents and narcissists pair up, the dancing experience sizzles with excitement – at least in the beginning. After many "songs," the enthralling and thrilling dance experience predictably transforms into drama, conflict, feelings of neglect and being trapped. Even with chaos and conflict, neither of the two spellbound dancers dares to end their partnership. Despite the tumultuous and conflict-laden nature of their relationship, neither of these two opposite, but dysfunctionally-compatible, dance partners feel compelled to "sit the dance out."

When a codependent and narcissist come together in their relationship, their dance unfolds flawlessly: The narcissistic partner maintains the lead and the codependent follows. Their roles seem natural to them because they have actually been practicing them their whole lives; the codependent reflexively gives up their power and since the narcissist thrives on control and power, the dance is perfectly coordinated. No one gets their toes stepped on. Typically, codependents give of themselves much more than their partners give back to them. As "generous" but bitter dance partners, they seem to be stuck on the dance floor, always waiting for the "next song," at which time they naively hope that their narcissistic partner will finally understand their needs. Codependents confuse caretaking and sacrifice with loyalty and love. Although they are proud of their unwavering dedication to the person they love, they end up feeling unappreciated and used. Codependents yearn to be loved, but because of their choice of dance partner, find their dreams unrealized. With the heartbreak of unfulfilled dreams, codependents silently and bitterly swallow their unhappiness.

Codependents are essentially stuck in a pattern of giving and sacrificing, without the possibility of ever receiving the same from their partner. They pretend to enjoy the dance, but really harbor feelings of anger, bitterness, and sadness for not taking an active role in their dance experience. They are convinced that they will never find a dance partner who will love them for who they are, as opposed to what they can do for them. Their low self-esteem and pessimism manifests itself into a form of learned helplessness that ultimately keeps them on the dance floor with their narcissistic partner.

The narcissist dancer, like the codependent, is attracted to a partner who feels perfect to them: Someone who lets them lead the dance while making them feel powerful, competent and appreciated. In other words, the narcissist feels most comfortable with a dancing companion who matches up with their self-absorbed and boldly selfish dance style. Narcissist dancers are able to maintain the direction of the dance because they always find partners who lack self-worth, confidence and who have low self-esteem – codependents. With such a well-matched companion, they are able to control both the dancer and the dance.

Although all codependent dancers desire harmony and balance, they consistently sabotage themselves by choosing a partner who they are initially attracted to, but will ultimately resent. When given a chance to stop dancing with their narcissistic partner and comfortably sit the dance out until someone healthy comes along, they typically choose to continue their dysfunctional dance. They dare not leave their narcissistic dance partner because their lack of self-esteem and self-respect makes them feel like they can do no better. Being alone is the equivalent of feeling lonely, and loneliness is too painful to bear.

Without self-esteem or feelings of personal power, the codependent is incapable of choosing mutually-giving and unconditionally-loving partners. Their choice of a narcissistic dance partner is connected to their unconscious motivation to find a person who is familiar – someone who is reminiscent of their powerless and, perhaps, traumatic childhood. Sadly, codependents are most likely children of parents who also flawlessly danced the dysfunctional codependent/narcissistic dance. Their fear of being alone, their compulsion to control and fix at any cost, and their comfort in their role as the martyr who is endlessly loving, devoted, and patient, is an extension of their yearning to be loved, respected, and cared for as a child.

Although codependents dream of dancing with an unconditionally loving and affirming partner, they submit to their dysfunctional destiny. Until they decide to heal the psychological wounds that ultimately compel them to dance with their narcissistic dance partners, they will be destined to maintain the steady beat and rhythm of their dysfunctional dance.

Through psychotherapy, and perhaps, a 12-step recovery program, the codependent can begin to recognize that their dream to dance the grand dance of love, reciprocity and mutuality is indeed possible. Through therapy and a change of lifestyle, codependents can build (repair) their tattered self-esteem. The journey of healing and transformation will bring them feelings of personal power and efficacy that will foster a desire to finally dance with someone who is willing and capable of sharing the lead, communicating their movements, and pursuing a mutual loving rhythmic dance.

CHAPTER 3

Emotional Manipulator & Codependent Relationship Dynamics

Language is directly impacted by our evolving culture, which especially includes the far-reaching influences of our popular media, the Internet, social networking, and other modern phenomena. Thanks to the proliferation of the Internet and the constant onslaught of technological advances, new words and phrases are "born" almost instantly. Hugely popular online phenomena like Facebook and Twitter are highly influential in crafting new words while redefining others. Likewise, mental health terminology is impacted by our evolving society. But with mental health terms, it is often a two-way street: As culture influences the terminology, so does terminology affect culture. Words like "dysfunctional," "denial," "projection," "OCD" and even "codependent" are now a part of our mainstream vocabulary. Although these crossover mental health terms have benefited the general public, over time, the overuse of them has resulted in a dilution of their original clinical meaning.

The manual that contains the accepted (by the American Psychiatric Association – APA) mental health diagnostic terms is the Diagnostic Statistic Manual for Mental Disorders or the DSM. The DSM provides a common language and standard criteria for the classification of mental or psychological disorders. Since mental health concepts are prone to subjective interpretations, a standardized, valid and research-based diagnostic guide is necessary – if not required. Considering that mental health fields are diverse, it is naturally impossible to have widespread agreement on all diagnostic terms, diagnostic categories, and their organization. Even though most mental health practitioners consider the DSM as the "bible" of mental health disorders, there is a widespread agreement that it has limitations. Although the DSM is a necessary clinical tool, it is as good as the times in which it was written, the culture it was written for and the current understanding (the science) of mental illness.

To stay relevant and modern, or to keep up with the evolving nature of our society, culture, politics, scientific or medical advances; the DSM has been revised on a semi-regular regular basis. Including the DSM-5, which will be published in May of 2013, it has been revised six times since it was first published in 1952. Over the last 60 years, with each DSM revision, diagnoses and diagnostic categories would be added, removed and/or updated as well as the formulations for the diagnostic process would be updated. As our society and the scientific understanding of mental health disorders have evolved, so has the DSM. Examples of the evolving nature of the DSM include:

- 1973: The diagnosis of "homosexuality" was removed.

- 1980: The diagnosis of "manic depression" was changed to "bipolar disorder."

- 1980: The "neurotic disorders" diagnostic category was eliminated.

- 1994: The diagnosis of "overanxious disorder of childhood" was changed to "generalized anxiety disorder."

- 2013: As reported by the American Psychiatric Association, Asperger's disorder will be removed.

To fully understand the core concepts in this book, it is necessary to provide standard or operational definitions for the diagnostic terms that I repeatedly use. This is especially necessary considering terms such as "codependency" and "emotional manipulator" are not included in the DSM. If these concepts and diagnostic terms (and others included in this book) are to be taken seriously, they should be clearly defined and scrubbed free of their jargonistic connotations. With clear definitions and subsequently better understanding of the terms and concepts, this book should have practical value to both clinicians and the general public.

"Dysfunctional" - What Does It Really Mean?

To start, the ubiquitous term "dysfunctional" is one of the most overused, misused, and commonly misunderstood mental health terms. Random House Dictionary dates the word back to 1915-1920. Its peak use was in the 1990's when it crossed over from the medical and clinical psychology fields to the mainstream vocabulary. To understand the manner in which the term is utilized in this book, it is first important to note that "healthy" and "normal" are the opposite of "dysfunctional." "Healthy or normal" individuals have problems, however, they rely on (and utilize) internal and external resources to solve them. In other words, healthy individuals seek help, assistance and/or professional services when the going gets rough. Moreover, these individuals have emotionally embedded resources to help them solve and/or adapt to their problems of difficult situations. Examples of internal resources are courage, humility, healthy vulnerability, insight and good judgment.

Because the term "dysfunctional relationship" is used throughout this book, it is important to provide a standard definition. *Dysfunctional relationships* are comprised of individuals who lack adequate mental or emotional health. These relationships are characterized by frequent or perpetual conflict which often goes unresolved. Dysfunctional relationship partners lack the ability, are unmotivated, or are powerless to interact with each other in a positive, empathic and affirming manner. They often interact with each other in a manner that is harmful and destructive to either or both parties. This pathological relationship is maintained by implicit and explicit rules and roles, which are unconsciously developed in order to avoid conflict or distress.

Dysfunctional relationship partners are typically unable to communicate in a manner that can facilitate effective problem solving. Often, either one or both individuals are resistant to outside resources to help with their problems. Lastly, dysfunctional relationships are perpetual; they persist by virtue of the fact that one or both partners do not or will not seek change or remediation.

Dysfunctional individuals typically ignore or deny that they have problems, do not have the psychological capacity to recognize or seek help for them, or do not believe they have the power or support to change them. Dysfunctional individuals often avoid seeking mental health services, resist them, and/or reluctantly or half-heartedly participate in them. If they do benefit from such outside interventions or services, in time, dysfunctional individuals often relapse into their former unhealthy behavioral, social, and/or psychological patterns. These individuals will likely return to therapy half-heartedly or, once again, resist seeking help. Since dysfunctional individuals resist seeking mental health services, reluctantly participate in them, or terminate them before they are completed, they perpetually experience their problems.

Codependents and Emotional Maninpulators

Although both codependency and the emotional manipulator disorders are indeed mental health or psychological disorders, neither is included in the current DSM. Just because the APA does not formally recognize a disorder, as evidenced by its inclusion in the DSM, does not mean it does not exist. Since the first publication of the DSM, it has become a common pattern that researchers and the APA have to catch up with what the clinicians have already learned or have demonstrated in the field.

Although codependency and the emotional manipulation disorders will be explored in detail in the following chapters, definitions for both terms will first be presented. The Merriam Webster's online dictionary defines codependency as: "A psychological condition or a relationship in which a person is controlled or manipulated by another who is affected with a pathological condition." This author defines codependency as follows: A disorder of selflessness, passivity and personal powerlessness.

Codependents are attracted to, or easily manipulated by, self-centered, self-consumed, and controlling individuals, i.e., narcissists or addicts. They tend to choose romantic partners who need them and who are compelled to control and dominate them. They often defer or place a lower priority on their own personal and emotional needs while being excessively preoccupied with the personal and emotional needs of others. Codependency can occur in any type of relationship.

Emotional manipulation is a newer diagnostic term that has recently been introduced in mental health seminars. Previously, the term was only understood by its denotative sense: manipulating a person's emotions. This author's definition for an emotional manipulator is as follows: an individual who has been diagnosed with one of three personality disorders – narcissistic, borderline, or antisocial personality disorder, and/or is chemically or behaviorally addicted. It is possible, however, to simultaneously have one of these three personality disorders and an addiction disorder. Although the emotional manipulation disorders are distinctly different from one another, they all share a narcissistic relationship orientation: They are entitled, grandiose, egotistic, and self-consumed.

Emotional manipulators interact with others from a perspective that is centrally focused on their needs. Their focus in relationships is usually on how people or situations impact them and their overwhelming need to be recognized and appreciated. Emotional manipulators typically exhibit an unrealistic, inflated or larger than life view of their own talents while devaluing the contributions or abilities of others. They tend to lack sensitivity and empathy in social situations and with individuals with whom they are in a relationship.

The main thesis of this book is that codependents and emotional manipulators are naturally attracted to each other because of their perfectly compatible dysfunctional inverse personalities. In relationships, codependents are pathologically-oriented toward the needs of others while downplaying or ignoring the importance of their own needs. Emotional manipulators are pathologically-oriented toward their own needs while dismissing or ignoring the needs of others. Because codependents seek to care for the needs of others and emotional manipulators seek to have their needs met, they are well-matched relationship partners.

As a direct result of their well-matched relationship orientations, codependents and emotional manipulators are irresistibly drawn to one another by what seems like an invisible magnetic-like force. When they first meet, they are enveloped in a magnetic and seductive energy force that initially fulfills their fantasy for true love, but later devolves into a painful seesaw of love/pain and hope/disappointment. As opposite but inversely matched dysfunctional individuals, they become compatible relationship partners. The same magnetic attraction force that brought them together also bonds them into a long-term and persistent relationship.

History is replete with examples of romantic couples who were irresistibly attracted to each other, not so much by what they saw, felt and thought, but more by an imperceptible but overwhelming magnetic-like attraction force. Anthony and Cleopatra (codependent-narcissist), John and Jacqueline Kennedy (narcissist-codependent), and Elvis and Priscilla Presley (narcissist-codependent), are just three of a countless number of famous couples whose relationship was driven by a magnetic-like love force.

When individuals with healthy emotional backgrounds meet, they are similarly pulled together by a formidable love force that is powered by their opposite and compatible personality traits. Unlike the codependent-emotional manipulator relationship, healthy lovers with well-matched personalities are able to build a loving, reciprocal and stable relationship. Their opposite relationship orientation or self-orientation is balanced, in that, neither individual is all about others or all about themselves.

In the most general sense, codependents are selfless individuals who are naturally oriented toward the love, respect and care (LRC) of others while ignoring or diminishing the importance of their own self-care.

On the contrary, emotional manipulators are selfish, self-absorbed and preoccupied with their own need for LRC. Because codependents are oriented in personal relationships toward the care of others and the emotional manipulator towards their own needs, they are considered opposite, compatible and dysfunctional relationship partners. As illustrated in the Dance essay, opposite dysfunctional partners make compatible relationship partners. Because the emotional manipulator and the codependent are compatible in a romantic relationship, they are likely to form an enduring or stable relationship. For the purpose of this book, stable is defined as able or likely to continue or last, firmly established, enduring or permanent. Stable, dysfunctional relationships are not desirable.

The codependent/emotional manipulator relationship is paradoxically considered a mutual and reciprocal relationship because both partners fulfill each other's emotional needs – the "caregiver" takes care of the "care-needer," while the "care-needer" is allowed to be narcissistically engrossed with his own life. Because both are inherently emotionally and psychologically deficient, they share a distorted belief that the other will make them feel whole. Instead of achieving the fantasy of personal "completeness," these partners create a "half relationship." The "relationship math" is simple: the addition of two "half individuals" create one person or a "half relationship." The dysfunctional level of this "half relationship" is in direct proportion to each other's psychological issues or mental health deficiencies. Emotionally unhealthy or psychologically deficient individuals can never create an emotionally healthy or psychologically stable relationship. Conversely, when two psychologically healthy parties come together in a romantic relationship, the result is a "whole relationship" comprising two interdependent individuals who affirm, respect and care equally for the other. With healthy partners, one plus one equals a whole relationship – comprising of two whole individuals.

The codependent-emotional manipulator relationship is naturally resistant to break-ups because neither appreciates or likes being alone. The state of being alone or not with their dysfunctional romantic partner, often triggers inherent and deeply embedded feelings of inadequacy and shame. Being alone simply brings them closer to their lonely emotional core. Since being alone makes them feel lonely, and loneliness is a painful and unbearable emotion, the relationship remains intact despite shared unhappiness and negative consequences (which are mostly for the codependent).

It is as if the codependents and emotional manipulators are addicted to each other. Like addicts who will do almost anything to get their fix, these two compulsively seek the pleasure of each other's company – something that feels great in the moment – but never lasts. It is as if they are each other's drug of choice – their preferred form of self-medication. Ultimately and predictably the compulsive nature of their relationship leads to a barrage of losses and consequences. Break-ups do not last, as the two cannot tolerate being without their "drugs." Getting back together after a break-up, therefore, is nothing more than a temporary "fix."

It is their opposite personalities or self-orientations that bind the codependent and emotional manipulator together in an enduring dysfunctional relationship. Despite their history of unhappiness, resentment, conflict and repeated breakups, the two remain together. Consequences, such as hurtful and protracted divorces, emotional harm to their children, spousal abuse, or restraining orders are often not enough to permanently separate these two. Paradoxically, their dysfunctional relationship provides them both with a distorted sense of security and safety. For the codependent and the emotional manipulator, pain and safety are often fused together.

A poem by one of my favorite poets, Rick Belden, exemplifies how these two are "fused at the wound."

fused at the wound
is it love or is it addiction
why not both
she knows tears + I know anger
together we almost made a whole person for a while
fused at the wound.

but our little house of lies isn't big enough to hold us now
she won't stand up for herself + I can't stand up
for both of us at the same time anymore
so we ride the broken lover's seesaw of staying + leaving
one foot in + one foot out
we dance in the kitchen like unloved children + wait
for fulfillment of old pain's expectations.

so anxious to leave   **so anxious to be left**
so anxious to be right   **so anxious to be hurt**

so anxious to be disappointed
so anxious to be alone again.

when this whole thing started
I wanted us to be immersed in each other
I wanted us to fix each other
I thought that was what people were supposed to do
I don't want that anymore
I don't need that anymore
but I still don't know
how to love someone I don't want to fix.

Reprinted by permission of the author, Rick Belden, from Iron Man Family Outing: Poems about Transition into a More Conscious Manhood, copyright 1990 by Rick Belden, http://rickbelden.com

If the codependent-emotional manipulator couple were to break up, one or both are likely to use guilt and manipulation as a tactic to reconnect. Insincere promises to change, reminders of good deeds, threats to relapse on a drug they are addicted to, or threats of emotional or physical harm to self or others, are some of the many manipulative ploys used to reconnect.

A common manipulative maneuver is triangulation, or using a third party, to facilitate reconciliation. The emotional manipulator, as a last ditch effort, may offer insincere but convincing promises to participate in psychotherapy. If the two do break up, it is typically short-lived, as the two are pulled back together by a magnetic-like dysfunctional love force. If the codependent and emotional manipulator do manage to decisively part ways, it is likely that both will unconsciously and unknowingly repeat their dysfunctional attraction pattern with their next romantic partner; someone who will feel exciting and different at first, but will ultimately have the same dysfunctional self-orientation as their previous partner. They will begin another dysfunctional relationship "dance" with a new partner, but will sadly dance to the same old song.

The Attraction of Similar and Opposite Individuals

All relationships are created and maintained by conscious and unconscious factors. The conscious preferences create the foundation on which the unconscious dynamics unfold. Typically, the allure of a prospective romantic partner deepens when similarities are shared or preferences are achieved. Research has confirmed what seems obvious: We are attracted to others who are similar to ourselves, whether it is because of their physical appearance, compatible attitude, peer group associations, political affiliation, social and cultural interests, hobbies or work preferences (Lydon, Jamieson & Zanna, 1988). It is common to be steadfast, and even stubborn, about our "must-have" relationship preferences.

As many of us already know, we desire a romantic relationship that is based on similarities, at least consciously. According to Susan Perry, author of *Loving in Flow: How the Happiest Couples Get and Stay That Way* (2003):

> **"People tend to look for almost a clone of themselves...
> they are very specific – too specific."**

Perry believes that people take their own inventory and compare it against possible mates. It is the consensus of researchers and clinicians alike that we all desire to find a compatible romantic companion who parallels our own values and personal preferences.

Our conscious preferences may mislead us to believe that we are the masters of our own relationship fate. Some of the conscious factors, or preferred traits, include, but are not limited to the following:

- Body type/characteristics

- Personality traits, e.g., serious, good sense of humor, etc.

- Religion

- Politics

- Ethnicity or race

- Education

- Sexual orientation and preferences

- The desire to have or not have children

- Regional preferences

- Recreational or social preferences

Although conscious choice and personal preferences are important in choosing a romantic partner, they are clearly secondary to unconscious preferences. "Chemistry" or an intense attraction experience occurs when both conscious and unconscious attraction dynamics come together to create a formidable hypnotic-like love force. With conscious and unconscious compatibility, the new and exciting romantic partnership is often beyond the conscious mind's capacity to regulate it. Although these deep feelings have a conscious "voice," they are often muted by the more powerful unconscious drive to merge emotionally, personally and sexually. The instinctive attraction experience results in a rush of powerful euphoric feelings that will convince any two star-crossed lovers that they are perfectly matched. Even when the signs of incompatibility, e.g., she is clingy and insecure (a codependent) and he talks all the time about himself and drinks too much (an alcoholic and narcissist), they still fall victim to their instinctual urges. This is the Human Magnet Syndrome.

According to many psychological theorists, we unconsciously gravitate toward relationships that are familiar and reminiscent of those experienced during our childhood. Without positive experiences in healthy relationships, both emotional manipulators and codependents ironically feel awkward and anxious when their romantic interest is healthy or emotionally balanced. Because both are unaware of the unconscious attraction dynamics, they often attribute this uncomfortable feeling to a lack of "chemistry." When emotional manipulators encounter healthy romantic partners, they feel annoyed and angered by that person's lack of patience and tolerance for their need to take front and center stage.

Moreover, the emotional manipulator is likely to be angered when their healthy date disagrees with them or does not share their similar thoughts or opinions on a variety of subjects. When codependents meet a prospective healthy lover, they feel anxious and nervous because they do not know how to participate in a mutual discussion or a dating situation that involves an equal amount of sharing, and giving. They simply do not know how to be an equal participant to a relationship. When pushed into a mutual and reciprocal relationship, codependents quickly move toward the "relationship exit door."

The Dysfunctional Love Trance

When a codependent and emotional manipulator consciously experience each other as attractive, they are magnetically drawn together because of their instinctive knowledge of dysfunctional environments. The feeling of attraction is extraordinarily deep – almost trance-like. These unconscious feelings of familiarity and comfort bring about feelings of safety and security. In actuality, the feelings of safety and security are only an illusion. They are directly connected to unconscious memories of their childhood dysfunctional relationship with their emotional manipulator parent.

Because codependents and emotional manipulators are dysfunctionally compatible, they experience intense excitement in the beginning phase of their relationship – almost like winning the lottery. The emotional manipulator's confidence, charm and need to be the center of attention will create a barrage of emotional fireworks for the codependent. The great listening skills, patience and accommodating nature of the codependent, as well as her unconditional acceptance, endless support and empathy will stoke the fire of the emotional manipulator's romantic fantasies. These two are likely to be instantly bonded by virtue of their compatible dysfunctional traits/personalities. Love will bloom as these two lovers experience their new relationship as a perfect fit.

Codependents instinctively react to the emotional manipulator's narcissistic traits in a positive manner, finding them intensely attractive, desirable and strangely familiar. They are reflexively attracted to narcissistic individuals who match up with their submissive, giving and sacrificial natures. Codependents appreciate, and are intensely attracted to, the emotional manipulator because they are enamored with what seems to them as positive and attractive personality traits, e.g. over-the-top confidence, articulate understanding of themselves, assertive or aggressive nature and their alluring sex appeal.

Codependents take great pride in their natural and well-developed abilities to be compassionate, patient and giving. Since codependents feel at ease and are comfortable in the role of sacrificing their own needs, while tending to the needs of others, they are naturally attracted to individuals who respond favorably to their caretaking role. Their selflessness and ability to absorb their partner's problems makes them a perfect sounding board for someone who is self-centered and self-consumed. They experience a form of pseudo self-esteem when they are in a relationship in which they feel needed and appreciated. It is as if they were born to help, solve and sacrifice. We will discover later in the book that this is not too far from the truth.

Codependents fall prey to the emotional manipulator's assertive, strong and commanding persona. During the attraction phase of the relationship, they are not aware that their new, exciting and intensely attractive romantic mate is actually a wolf in sheep's clothing – an emotional manipulator. Because the codependent is beguiled by their prospective partner's charismatic personality, they are unable to recognize the potential harm that these individuals can cause them. Despite the fact they do not intentionally seeking narcissistic romantic partners, they unfortunately find themselves perpetually in their company.

Through the eyes of the codependent, an emotional manipulator's inherent narcissism is experienced as an appealing trait. Instead of appearing arrogant, controlling and self-centered, emotional manipulators are experienced as confident, assertive, sexy and charming, but with an "edge." Not only are codependents attracted to their quirky arrogant and self-aggrandizing personality, they also feel strangely emotionally balanced by it. Feeling complete, with their well-matched and compatible mate, the codependent becomes locked into a dysfunctionally comforting and potentially permanent romantic relationship.

Like their codependent partners, emotional manipulators are naturally attracted to individuals who are compatible with their unique, but dysfunctional, personality traits. They instantly feel comfortable, safe and familiar with prospective lovers who respond to their narcissistic traits as desirable and captivating. Emotional manipulators are especially attracted to individuals who appreciate and idealize them for their stories of adversity and struggles while also feeling compelled to take care of them. When around healthy people, they often feel misunderstood, underappreciated and judged. However, when a prospective romantic partner is attracted to them, especially because of their unique self-centered and egotistic traits, they experience a wave of euphoric excitement. They experience emotional freedom when they do not have to worry about upsetting someone because of their narcissistic personality traits, which they don't recognize, but also deny having.

The caring nature of the codependent, combined with their characteristic empathy, unconditional acceptance, patience and support almost always stokes the emotional manipulator's romantic desires. The emotional manipulator naturally considers the codependent's selfless and others-oriented self-orientation as intensely attractive and desirable. It is usually a "love at first sight" experience when they meet their well-matched and compatible partner. They experience feelings of safety and familiarity which subsequently leads them into a trance-like attraction dynamic that ultimately creates distorted feelings of security and an intense romantic attraction. Since the emotional manipulator is "built" to be attracted to a codependent, the relationship will likely withstand the test of time, therefore becoming *dysfunctionally stable*.

In the beginning of the relationship, both the codependent and the emotional manipulator are swept up in what may seem like a dream relationship – true love. The intensity of the attraction is formidable. It is inescapably alluring and enthralling. Once settled into their quickly formed relationship, neither partner could endure a separation, as the two inherently unhealthy partners complete each other's dysfunction. The two are not only "head-over-heels" in love with each other; their perfectly compatible personalities lock them into a quasi-permanent dysfunctional relationship.

On a conscious level, each experiences the other as their fantasy person, or soul mate. However, far from their conscious awareness are deeper and darker feelings of dysfunctional familiarity. The unconscious feelings of familiarity compel both individuals to repeat the catch-22 relationship pattern of their childhood – needing to be loved by a person who is characteristically unable to love them or anyone else. More specifically, they will be compelled to repeat a version of their childhood relationship with their emotional manipulator parent. The codependent will do anything to get their partner to love them while the emotional manipulator will do anything to ensure their own safety and needs. This pattern will be discussed in detail in chapters 7 and 8.

The Power of Limerence

It is part of human nature to experience tremendously powerful personal, emotional and physical sensations in the beginning of a romantic relationship - especially if there is strong physical attraction. With highly compatible relationships, each individual initially feels involuntary surges of intense and overwhelming personal, emotional and sexual excitement. This intense romantic attraction, or *limerence,* creates overpowering and obsessive cravings to seek the intensely stimulating company of their new love.

According to Dorothy Tennov (1999), "Limerence…can be experienced as intense joy or as extreme despair, depending on whether the feelings are reciprocated. Basically, it is the state of being completely carried away by unreasoned passion or love, even to the point of addictive-type behavior." Simply defined, limerence is an overwhelming, obsessive need to have one's feelings reciprocated.

Symptoms of Limerence (D. Tennov 1979)

- Intrusive thinking about the limerent object (LO)
- Acute longing for reciprocation of attention and affection
- Mood fluctuations based on LO's actions
- Can only feel it with one person at a time
- All-consuming obsession that the LO will relieve the pain
- Preoccupation (fear) with rejection
- Incapacitating and uncomfortable shyness in the beginning of the relationship
- Intensification of limerence through adversity
- An aching "heart" (in the chest) when there are doubts
- Buoyancy ("walking on air") with reciprocation
- Intense obsessions demotivate the person from other responsibilities (friends, family, work)
- Emphasis is placed on positive attributes of the LO, while ignoring the negative

In the beginning of the relationship, the love-struck, or *limerent,* couple is compelled by extreme emotional, physical and sexual urges to merge into a romantic relationship, which they believe will make them feel whole and complete. Although sexual attraction plays a key role in the development of the bond, by itself it does not account for the burning emotional/relationship desires evident in the limerent couple. Sex, however, almost always "seals the deal" and drives this hypnotic limerence/love force into deeper and more consuming levels.

When the codependent and the emotional manipulator first meet, their shared limerence creates off-the-charts infatuation that ultimately resembles Obsessive Compulsive Disorder (OCD). When apart, neither can stop thinking about the other, nor do they feel much like eating or sleeping. Each partner is obsessed by the other; neither can control their non-stop thoughts about the new relationship. The couple simultaneously experience powerful body sensations that may make them feel like they are floating on air. The perfect feelings created when they are together quickly bring these two into a close and enmeshed romantic relationship.

The drug-like feelings responsible for limerence are primarily caused by brain chemicals, primarily the neurotransmitter dopamine. When a person experiences the "high" of new love or intense attraction, neurons are activated in the reward system of the brain which releases a flood of dopamine. At the same time, the hormone norepinephrine is released, which is responsible for an increase in blood pressure, sweaty palms and the pounding heart experience. Simultaneously, levels of the neurotransmitter serotonin are lowered or inhibited, which stimulates obsessive and compulsive behaviors and thought processes. When the codependent and emotional manipulator fall in love, it is like being high on very potent intoxicating drugs and experiencing a serious case of OCD.

"Love at first sight" is one of the most common themes in movies, novels and songs, replete with the naïve woman (codependent) falling for the edgy and aggressive (emotional manipulator) "bad boy." Society's entertainment catalogs are chock full of love stories involving codependents and emotional manipulators. One such example is the love story of John Dillinger, a notorious American bank robber, and his caretaking girlfriend, Billie Frechette. Dillinger was considered a ruthless and coldhearted psychopath who was a celebrity of sorts. The media was laced with accounts of his audacious and larger than life personality. Dillinger would have been considered an emotional manipulator, as evidenced by his egotistic, grandiose and sociopathic disregard for laws and people. More specifically, he would have most likely been diagnosed with antisocial personality disorder.

Ms. Frechette likely would have been considered a codependent, as evidenced by her relationships with incarcerated criminals, together with her caretaking personality and habitual tendency to sacrifice her own personal and emotional welfare for narcissistic men. Before meeting Dillinger, Frechette was married to a man who was sentenced to prison for committing mail robbery. Unlike Bonnie Parker, Clyde Barrow's active accomplice, Frechette was not compelled to be Dillinger's partner in crime. She made purchases for him, such as clothing and cars, but primarily she performed the duties of a housewife. She was a loyal companion to John Dillinger until her arrest in April 1934, and subsequent trial, conviction and sentencing for harboring a federal fugitive.

Billie Frechette, like other codependents, was entranced by her emotional manipulator's toughness, independence and over-the-top confidence. Dillinger's aggression, bravado, and all-consuming feelings of importance and superiority were traits which Billie couldn't resist. According to Ms. Frechette, she couldn't help but to fall instantly in love with John Dillinger.

I'll never forget that. It happened the way things do in the movies. I was 25 years old and I wasn't any different from all the other girls that were 25 years old. Nothing that happened to me up to that time had amounted to anything. Then I met John and everything was changed. I started a new kind of life. There was something in those eyes that I will never forget. They were piercing and electric, yet there was an amused carefree twinkle in them too. They met my eyes and held me hypnotized for an instant. He just stared at me and smiled a little bit with the corner of his mouth. His eyes seemed to go all the way through me.

(Schroeder, 2011)

What would have happened if Billie Frechette was psychologically healthy when she met John Dillinger? Since there would not have been emotional/psychological compatibility, she would likely have been instantly repulsed by Dillinger's narcissistic and aggressive personality. When first encountering Dillinger, Billie would have felt what some might call a "creepy feeling." She would have consciously and unconsciously have recognized him as untrustworthy and potentially dangerous. Conversely, if a healthy person met Billie, they would have experienced her as insecure, needy, and unable to decide what she wanted or how she felt – definitely not emotionally alluring.

Often, in an instant, highly opposite but compatible codependents and emotional manipulators fall "in love" (experience limerence) and quickly become enmeshed and dependent upon each other. The soul mate dream quickly devolves into the "cell-mate" reality. In the beginning, they can't live without each other and later… they can't live with each other. The honeymoon phase never lasts very long. It is inevitable that shortly after the two dysfunctional lovers meet, the feelings of limerence will be replaced by conflict, chaos and misery (more so for the codependent).

CHAPTER 4

"The Odd but Natural Couple"

She drives a Mercedes, he rides a Harley; she's an athlete, he's a bookworm; he's a Republican, she's a Democrat... Have you ever wondered why some of us have personal friends whom we appreciate, like, or even love, but who are the same people who are likely to annoy us the most? If an attorney and a community-based social worker marry or an obsessively clean and a disorganized friend become roommates, shouldn't it then result in an incompatible and unstable relationship? Not necessarily.

Just as with romantic relationships, opposite personality types are also naturally drawn together into compatible and enduring personal friendships. We tend to choose people who appear to give us the very qualities we think we are lacking (Reik, 2011). Compatible opposite friendships or odd but natural "couples" work because their opposite personality traits gel. Despite distinctly differing opinions and moments of conflict, each half of the odd but natural couple is "glued" to the other half because their appreciation and valuing of the other outweighs their frustrations and annoyances.

Not all opposite personalities are compatible in a relationship. When opposite and different personality traits are not balanced or compatible, the individuals are not likely to form a friendship. If they do, it will predictably be unstable or short-lived. Without the compatibility of balanced opposite personality traits, the relationship will generally not be experienced as mutually beneficial and rewarding. In other words, without a "payoff" for their differences, the romantic or personal association will undoubtedly not last. These are the friendships that typically end with conflict or the relationship just fades away.

The Inverse Attraction Dynamic

The natural attraction to opposite personality traits is an *inverse process*. The Merriam-Webster dictionary defines inverse as: "opposite in order, nature or effect." The inverse attraction dynamic is based on proportionally opposite or dichotomous personality traits. Friends who are opposite, but compatible, or who are an "odd but natural couple," are attracted to each other because their differences correspond or match with each other. A proportionally balanced inverse attraction is paradoxical in nature, as it requires perfectly matched dissimilarities. For example, a compulsive clean-freak may be attracted to a disorganized and messy person. Although both might be annoyed by each other's perceived shortcomings, they adapt because of the inherent benefits of their compatibly different personality traits.

As much as compatible extreme opposites are attracted to each other, so are compatible mild opposites. For the mild opposite bond to be successful, there needs to be a balance in the inverse or diametrically opposite personality traits. To illustrate, a mildly shy and socially awkward person and a moderately extroverted and socially confident individual may likely form a mutually satisfying and compatible friendship. In this "odd but natural" friendship, the differences may result in occasional mild feelings of discomfort or conflict, but both will ultimately feel safe, comfortable and cared for within the relationship. The shy-gregarious combination will enhance the relationship as long as both individuals are benefitting from it. Such a friendship is likely to survive the test of time.

Examples of personality traits that are dichotomously opposite, but potentially compatible, include:

- Thinking versus feeling[4]

- Introverted versus extroverted[5]

- Private versus public

- Career-oriented versus home-oriented

- Tidy versus messy

- Generous versus thrifty

---

[4] One of the Myers Briggs Personality Test matching personality dichotomies.
[5] Another Myers Briggs Personality Test matching personality dichotomies.

Famous Odd Couples

Odd but natural couples constitute some of the most unlikely relationship pairs. Perhaps the most famous of these was portrayed in Neil Simon's Broadway play, two movies and TV sitcom, *The Odd Couple*. Felix Unger and Oscar Madison's oddly compatible relationship is introduced in the show's opening sequence.

"On November 13, Felix Unger was asked to remove himself from his place of residence; that request came from his wife. Deep down, he knew she was right, but he also knew that someday he would return to her. With nowhere else to go, he appeared at the home of his childhood friend, Oscar Madison. Several years earlier, Madison's wife had thrown him out, requesting that he never return. Can two divorced men share an apartment without driving each other crazy?"

The answer is a resounding YES! The story line of *The Odd Couple* was based on the odd, but very funny, rapport between Oscar Madison, a sports writer who was free spirited and very messy, and Felix Unger, a fashion photographer who was uptight and compulsively clean. Even though the two roommates had diametrically opposite beliefs, values and lifestyles, they were able to overcome their differences while remaining committed and loyal friends.

Who would have thought that an uptight, compulsive neat freak would be able to live with a roommate who was unkempt, gruff, laid-back and incorrigibly messy? "The two men – one divorced and one estranged and neither quite sure why their marriages fell apart – move in together to save money for alimony and suddenly discover they're having the same conflicts and fights they had in their marriages." (*Kassel, 2012*) The show's laughs were derived from the follies of these seemingly opposite, but ultimately compatible, roommates.

Even in real life, Walter Matthau (Oscar) and Jack Lemmon (Felix) were an "odd couple." Despite their differences, they were life-long friends, appearing in ten movies together. The biographies of these men illustrate their different backgrounds. Walter Matthau was born to Russian Jewish peddler parents, on the lower east side of New York City. As a boy, he was introduced to acting when he played bit parts in a Yiddish theatre. After high school, Walter joined the Army, and, in World War II, was a radioman-gunner on bombers.

According to Jack Lemmon's *New York Times* obituary, "Mr. Lemmon was a child of privilege who was destined for Harvard. Jack Lemmon, Mr. Matthau once said, 'is a clean-cut, well-scrubbed Boston choirboy with quiet hysteria seeping out of every pore (2001).' Jack Lemmon went to college at Harvard University where he was in the Navy ROTC and the Dramatic Club. After Harvard, Lemmon joined the Navy, receiving V-12 training and serving as an officer."

Another TV "odd couple" whose opposite personality traits are perfectly balanced is Penny and Dr. Leonard Hofstadter of the CBS sitcom, *The Big Bang Theory*. As across-the-hall neighbors, Penny and Leonard become an unlikely romantic pair. Penny, from Omaha, Nebraska, is a high school graduate, an aspiring but not very talented actress, and a waitress. Leonard, conversely, is from New Jersey, has a Ph.D. from Princeton University and is a successful experimental physicist. Penny is socially outgoing, assertive, carefree and flirtatious, if not promiscuous, while Leonard is socially awkward, geeky, anxious, insecure, and a prude.

Both Penny and Leonard find themselves romantically attracted to personality types that often leave them feeling empty and unloved. Penny's history is of short-term sexual relationships with men who treat her as a sexual object. Leonard has only been involved with a few women, who, like himself, tend to be nerdy, overly intellectual and ultimately uninteresting. Penny and Leonard's unusual friendship evolved into a romantic relationship – providing many funny moments.

Despite Penny and Leonard's opposite qualities, their relationship worked. The success of this relationship, much like that of Oscar and Felix, was due to their dichotomously opposite, but compatible, personalities. Their "odd but natural" relationship succeeded because Penny's socially fluent, spontaneous, laid back and communicative personality offset Leonard's hyper-analytical, socially inept, insecure, shy, and anal-retentive side. If Penny and Leonard's inverse personality traits did not provide a benefit for each other, the relationship would have never worked (and would not have been good comedy).

As presented in this chapter, opposites do attract and can have a healthy relationship. Finding a friend or lover who perfectly opposes our own personality could be another secret to a life-long relationship.

As much as the "Codependency Don't Dance" essay and its metaphorical concepts has helped my clients better understand their dysfunctional relationship patterns, its practical use was limited. With the overwhelming positive feedback I received on the Dance essay, I was compelled to further develop my hypotheses about dysfunctional relationship patterns. I would ultimately develop a commonsensical and practical psychological theory that would explain the ubiquitous and seemingly hard to understand codependent/emotional manipulator attraction patterns. My collection of explanations and hypotheses would ultimately culminate into The Continuum of Self Theory; a theory that would change the way that many a therapist and client would look at dysfunctional relationship patterns.

The Continuum of Self Theory would become an intuitively comprehensible theoretical formulation that would account for the habitual and dysfunctional nature of the codependents/emotional manipulator relationship. It would be a universal theory, as it would apply to all individuals, ranging from those who are psychologically unhealthy to those who are completely balanced and psychologically healthy. Moreover, the theory would account for the malleable nature of the human condition, as we all are inherently capable of growing and learning from our mistakes, overcoming difficult personal conditions, and with professional help, overcoming the powerful and seemingly indelible forces of our unconscious mind.

The continuum of self theory has helped my clients to better understand the dysfunctional nature of their current relationships while inspiring them to move beyond their habitual dysfunctional relationship patterns. It has also helped them to better understand the unconscious forcers that directed their relationship behavior. Additionally, it would become indispensable to my psychotherapy work, as it served as a simple explanatory "blueprint" for interpersonal and relational health. It has also become a road map of sorts, as it has helped my clients to conceptualize their current relational health, identify their progress (or lack of progress), and to have a clearer idea of their ultimate relationship "destination."

The Self-Orientation Concept

The continuum of self theory was designed to represent a person's "self-orientation." The term, self-orientation represents a distinctly human personality characteristic. It defines the manner in which a person expresses or does not express their emotional or psychological needs when in a romantic relationship. There are only two self-orientation types: the first is the "other" self-orientation. This is an individual who tends to be naturally and reflexively oriented toward the needs of others. The second is the "self" self-orientation. This is a person who is naturally and reflexively oriented toward his own wants – or the needs of self.

The continuum of self measures the full range of the self-orientation possibilities. The dichotomous self-orientations are measured in degrees: from healthy to dysfunctional. On the far ends of the continuum lie the most dysfunctional manifestations of the others and self self-orientation. The middle point on the continuum represents a self-orientation that is equally balanced between the needs of others and the needs of self. In my seminars, I sometimes joke and call this the "mythically balanced person." Codependents have the most severe and dysfunctional form of the "others" self-orientation. Conversely, emotional manipulators have the most severe and dysfunctional form of the "self" self-orientation.

The continuum of self theory was designed to quantitatively and qualitatively represent a person's self-orientation. As a *quantitative* tool, it demonstrates a relationship attraction dynamic through the use of basic arithmetic – addition and subtraction of positive and negative numbers. Through the addition of each person's continuum of self numerical value, it is possible to identify psychological compatibility of two romantic partners. The "mathematical" nature of the theory also illustrates when a relationship is stable, or, in other words, if it will endure. The continuum concept is ideal as it also *qualitatively* represents the full range of personality and relationship possibilities, according to the self-orientation construct it measures.

The Love, Respect, and Care Ratio

The continuum of self theory suggests that all people are consciously and unconsciously attracted to romantic partners who have an opposite, but proportionally balanced, self-orientation. A person who is oriented toward the needs of others or the *love, respect and care **(LRC) needs of others*** will naturally gravitate, or be magnetically attracted to a partner who has an opposite self-orientation – toward the ***LRC needs of self.*** It would then be logical to assume that individuals with opposite relationship orientations or self-orientations would not only be attracted to each other, but also feel emotionally balanced out by the other. These opposite but compatible individuals would bond in a relationship which would likely be enduring and resistant to change.

Codependents almost always provide abundant amounts of LRC to others while not actively seeking or requiring the same from others. In other words, codependents are naturally oriented toward fulfilling the LRC needs of others while devaluing and ignoring the same for themselves. Conversely, emotional manipulators are almost always more motivated to satiate their own LRC needs, while devaluing, ignoring and neglecting the LRC needs of their romantic partners. Codependents and emotional manipulators are polar opposite personality types, as represented on the continuum of self.

When a codependent and an emotional manipulator meet, and they are consciously attracted to each other,[6] their opposite but compatible self-orientations will result in a passionate experience of mutual attraction, or intense "chemistry." The powerful attraction experience is fueled by their compatible, but opposite, self-orientations. Even with obvious personal differences, such as "he's unemployed" or "she drinks too much," an unconscious attraction dynamic or perceived "chemistry" draws the two into a steamy "dance" of infatuation, intrigue and sexual desire. I call this attraction dynamic the Human Magnet Syndrome.

---

[6] Attracted by similarities: similar appreciations, physical attraction, cultural, ethnic and/or religious background, education, education, career aspirations, etc.

We are all consciously attracted to romantic partners who fit our own bullet list of attractive and desirable traits. Moreover, we are unconsciously attracted to individuals who inversely match up with our unique self-orientation. Like two oppositely charged magnets, we are drawn to romantic partners with an opposite but compatible self-orientation. If we have an "others" self-orientation, we will naturally gravitate toward individuals whom we will love, respect and care for more than we do the same for ourselves. If "self" self-oriented, we are naturally attracted to individuals who will give us more LRC than we will give to them. As will be discussed later in the book, our unconscious attraction patterns represent deep-seated emotional needs, which can be traced back to the manner in which we were parented as young children.

A codependent and an emotional manipulator constitute a balanced relationship because of their *inverse* relationship to each other. To illustrate, if one partner's self-orientation changes quantitatively, and the relationship is to stay balanced or stable, then there will need to be a corresponding change in the other partner self-orientation. Relationship stability, therefore, is maintained by corresponding self-orientation shifts. If one partner becomes healthier, as evidenced by a healthier balance between LRC given and received, and the other partner responds with similar growth, then the relationship will be stable – while becoming healthier. However, if the partner of the healthier individual does not want to change/grow, then stress is placed on the relationship. The stress will either lead to a breakdown of the relationship or create pressure for the healthier partner to regress to former levels of dysfunctional functioning. Failure to maintain a balanced inverse bond may result in the failure of a relationship.

Opposite Personality Possibilities

The self-orientation is considered a *dichotomous personality construct,* because it is divided into two parts – a comfort in giving or a comfort in taking. Codependent and emotional manipulation disorders are opposite and mutually exclusive personality possibilities that are understood as extreme contrary self-orientations. They are the polar opposites of a self-orientation dichotomy. In other words, codependency is the antithesis of an emotional manipulation disorder, and vice versa. As differing and dichotomous personality types that are measured by one construct (self-orientation), codependency and an emotional manipulator disorder can be represented on opposing sides of the continuum of self.

The Oxford Dictionary defines a continuum as "a continuous sequence or progression of values in which adjacent elements are not perceptibly different from each other, although the extremes are quite distinct." Because continua involve gradual quantitative transitions without abrupt changes or discontinuities, they are commonly used to describe psychological concepts. The most well-known psychological continua are the drug or alcohol abuse or depression varieties. The drug or alcohol abuse continuum begins with experimentation and ends with death by chronic drug abuse or overdose. The depression continuum begins with slight, imperceptible sadness and ends with severe, and potentially suicidal, depression. Continua are ideal measurement tools as they reduce complicated psychological processes into more simplistic, concrete and linear explanations.

Because of its linear and bi-directional nature, a continuum aptly represents the inverse and dichotomous properties of interacting self-orientations. Since the dichotomous and inverse self-orientations can be represented as a set of numbers ranging from negative five to zero or positive five to zero – zero being the midpoint – a continuum is an ideal conceptual and descriptive tool.

Continuum of Self Values

The continuum of self utilizes 11 numerical values, or continuum of self values (CSVs), to represent the full-range of self-orientation possibilities. At the center of the continuum is a CSV of zero. The zero represents a hypothetical perfect balance of one's "self" and "other" orientation. The highest number to the left of zero is negative five, which represents codependency – a self-orientation that is defined by the complete focus on the needs of others while neglecting one's own needs. The highest number to the right of zero is a positive five, which represents one of the emotional manipulator disorders – a self-orientation defined by the complete focus on one's own needs at the exclusion of others. The self-orientations progress in varying degrees of severity; a negative or positive five (-5/+5) is the most severe or pathological. The CSVs increase or decrease in a series of single digits, i.e., zero to negative five or zero to positive five. The closer the CSV is to zero, the more a person is able to "give and take" when in a romantic relationship. The further from zero, the more a person adopts a relationship pattern of selflessness or selfishness.

The zero value does not signify an absence of self-orientation. Instead, it represents a person who demonstrates an equal amount of "self-care" and "other-care" when in a relationship. The zero point, the middle of the continuum, represents an *exact* balance of love, respect and care (LRC), *given* and *received*. It is possible, but not common (in my experience), for a person to have a zero or neutral CSV. Although having a zero would be ideal, in reality, the vast majority fall somewhere on one side or the other of the continuum.

In an effort to illustrate the full range of self-orientations, this author has included a list of general personality types that are typically associated with each of the continuum of self values (CSVs). This list illustrates the full range of general personality possibilities according to the Continuum of Self Theory's self-orientation concept. This CSV list will provide a basic and general illustration for each of the 11 CSVs, according to the Continuum of Self Theory. It is not intended to be used as a measurement tool.

Examples of Each Continuum of Self Value (CSV)

-5 CSV: A codependent is completely absorbed with the love, respect and care (LRC) needs of others, while completely ignoring and devaluing their own. This category of individual is often powerless, unable and/or unwilling to seek LRC from his romantic partner.

-4 CSV: A person with codependent tendencies. He is almost always focused on the LRC needs of others while only intermittently seeking to have his own LRC needs reciprocated or fulfilled. This person is able, albeit unmotivated, fearful and/or inexperienced in seeking LRC from his romantic partner. He often chooses not to ask others to fulfill his LRC needs, as he doesn't want to upset others or cause conflict. If asking for some semblance of LRC from his partner, he does so nervously and with distinct feelings of guilt or neediness.

-3 CSV: A person who identifies with his caring and giving nature. He is predominately focused on the LRC needs of others, while often diminishing, delaying or excusing away the fulfillment of his own needs. This person's identity and reputation is fused with his helping and caretaking nature. He is typically in relationships in which there is an imbalance between his partner's and his own LRC needs – giving much more LRC to his partner than receiving. This individual is capable of setting boundaries in relationships while also asking for what he needs, however, he tends to feel guilty or needy when setting such boundaries or when asking for help from others.

-2 CSV: One involved in relationships in which his caretaking identity is valued and appreciated, but not exploited. He enjoys relationships with others in which he provides ample amounts of LRC, without wanting equal amounts reciprocated. He is able to ask for what he wants or needs from others, although is slightly uncomfortable doing so. He is comfortable with a partner who needs more LRC than he is willing to give in return. He is able to set boundaries and ask for what he needs when the LRC balance goes beyond his comfort level. He might experience mild feelings of guilt or neediness when asking his partner to meet his own LRC needs. As much as is possible, he avoids individuals who are narcissistic, exploitative or manipulative.

-1 CSV: A person with a healthy balance between loving, respecting and caring for self and others. He typically seeks life experiences and relationships in which he is able to satisfy his own LRC needs. He tends to participate and appreciate relationships that are based on a reciprocal and mutual distribution of LRC. Although he derives meaning and happiness when helping and caring for others, he does not tolerate a selfish or self-centered romantic partner. He often enjoys caring for others, but does not identify himself as a caretaker or helper. He does not experience guilt or feelings of neediness when asking for LRC from others.

0 CSV: A person who participates in relationships where there is an equal distribution of LRC given and received. He easily asks for what he needs from his partner, while being open to his partner's LRC needs. With his LRC-balanced relationships, he can easily fluctuate between being the recipient and giver of LRC.

+1 CSV: A person with a healthy balance between loving, respecting and caring for self and others. He tends to participate and appreciate relationships that are based on a reciprocal and mutual distribution of LRC. This individual values personal and professional goals and ambitions, which he confidently pursues. Although he derives meaning and happiness through the pursuit of his own goals and ambitions, he is also cognizant of the necessity to love, respect and care for his romantic partner. He effortlessly provides LRC to his romantic partner when necessary or requested. He may identify with both the role of a caretaker or helper while wanting to fulfill his own goals and ambitions.

+2 CSV: A person who prefers to be involved in relationships in which the pursuit to fulfill his own ambitions, desires and goals is encouraged and supported. In a romantic relationship, he actively seeks attention, appreciation and affirmation. Although he is a go-getter and may be consumed with "getting the spotlight," he is willing and able to fulfill his partner's needs. He is neither exploitative nor selfish. As an individual who is more oriented toward his own LRC needs, he periodically forgets about the inequity of LRC distribution in the relationship. He responds favorably and non-reactively when his partner asks for higher levels of LRC. Although he can be comfortable in a caretaking role, he doesn't maintain it.

+3 CSV: A mildly selfish and self-centered individual. He is predominately focused on the LRC needs of self, while often diminishing, delaying or excusing away the fulfillment of his partner's needs. This person's identity and reputation is fused with his need for attention, validation and recognition. He identifies with the persona of the go-getter and success-driven individual. He is typically in relationships where there is an imbalance in the distribution of LRC needs, expecting or taking more LRC than giving. If confronted about the LRC inequality, he may get defensive, but will be able to make corrections. He can modulate or control his self-centered and seemingly selfish attributes. Although he may be perceived as self-consumed and self-centered, he is willing and able to love, respect and care for his partner; he just needs frequent reminders.

+4 CSV: A narcissistic individual. This individual is absorbed and preoccupied with the LRC needs of self, while rarely seeking to fulfill the LRC needs of others. He comes across as being entitled, self-absorbed and self-centered, as he is driven to seek LRC from others, while giving very minimal amounts of the same in return. He is comfortable with the LRC disparity, believing his needs are more important than his partner's. Although this person is overtly narcissistic, he is still able to give nominal levels of LRC to others. If confronted about the LRC inequities, he will characteristically get angry and defensive and is quick to justify his actions. He, however, does not experience a narcissistic injury or exhibit narcissistic rage when confronted.

+5 CSV: An emotional manipulator. Unable and unmotivated to love, respect and care for others. He is consumed with fulfilling his own LRC needs with no intention of reciprocating. He has great difficulty in exhibiting empathy, unconditional positive regard or love. When he does give LRC to others, it is typically conditional, with strings attached. He is not able to comprehend or accept his pathological levels of narcissism. When confronted about the LRC imbalances, he will often strike back with either direct or passive aggression.

The Continuum of Self is a linear representation of a person's self-orientation. Lower negative and lower positive values, typically indicate an elevated level of relational and mental health. Conversely, higher negative and higher positive CSVs typically indicate lower levels of relational and mental health. To illustrate, mildly "others"- and mildly "self"- oriented individuals, a (-2) and (+2) CSV pairing, would represent two healthy people who, when paired in a romantic relationship, would create a healthier, mutually-loving, respectful and caring relationship than a relationship comprising (-4) and (+4) CSV. The lower CSV couple is able to ebb and flow in the way they approach their LRC needs. Moreover, the lower CSV partners are able to ask for what they need without causing resentment or conflict in their relationship. Despite a mild level of self-orientation inequality, both partners are able to give the other the amount of LRC that they need and desire. This is a healthy relationship.

In this book, the term *stable* is used as a quantitative descriptor of a relationship. A *stable* relationship is resistant to break-up. An unstable relationship is likely to either not go beyond the initial stages or will likely end when conflict or discord is present. *Stable* does not represent qualitative elements of a relationship, like whether or not it is considered healthy or dysfunctional. According to the continuum of self theory, a relationship is considered *stable* when the two individuals have inversely matched (opposite) self-orientations. In other words, relationship stability is achieved when the negative and positive CSVs of each individual equals a zero sum. A *"zero sum relationship"* describes this quantitative state of relationship stability. To illustrate, a moderately others-oriented individual, a (-3) CSV, is likely to form an emotionally stable and lasting relationship with a person who is moderately oriented toward their own needs, a (+3) CSV. Therefore, the (-3) and (+3) CSVs "equal" a zero sum relationship – one that is balanced and *stable*.

The Zero Sum Relationship

The zero sum relationship is not a *qualitative* representation of mental health. In actuality, the mental health of a relationship is directly proportional to the degree of the partner's negative or positive CSV values. Healthier relationships are comprised of partners who share inversely matched lower or mild CSVs. With lower matching CSVs, a couple is likely to want to and be able to participate in a "give and take" process. Although one partner is more oriented toward the needs of others and the other is more oriented toward the needs of self, both are able to be reciprocal and mutual in the relationship. It should be noted that there is a range of healthy zero sum relationships, as there is a rich diversity in the manner in which CSV-matched healthy individuals relate to one another.

Conversely, unhealthy or dysfunctional relationships are composed of partners who share inversely matched higher CSVs. The matching of higher inverse CSVs results in a disproportionate exchange of LRC – given and received. Clearly one person, the emotional manipulator, is getting all the LRC while the other, the codependent, is giving it.

The following vignette illustrates a healthy relationship with compatible self-orientations:

A psychologically healthy stay-at-home mother, who loves to volunteer, married a psychologically healthy and stable corporate executive, who, with the support of his wife, works long hours to build his stature and reputation in the family business. The wife has a CSV of (-2) and the husband has a CSV of (+2). With inverse CSVs, they both feel loved by the other and participate in a mutually and reciprocally loving relationship. They are happy and secure in their relationship.

By contrast, the following vignette illustrates an unhealthy zero sum relationship:

A codependent[7] man, with a CSV of (-5), is married to a woman with narcissistic personality disorder and a CSV of (+5). The codependent husband is deeply insecure, needy and compliant. He reluctantly agreed to stay home and raise the children while his narcissistic wife, an unsuccessful salesperson, insisted on being the family's sole provider. Because of his fear of enraging his overly sensitive and defensive wife, he avoids confronting her about her selfish and rigid role expectations. He, therefore, suppresses his resentment and anger for her and complies with his wife's narcissistic demands. As a (+5) narcissist, the wife will not even consider his needs unless they make her feel better about herself. If confronted about her narcissism, she will react harshly and even punitively to her codependent husband. This couple will stay together, despite their dysfunctional marriage. Neither would dare leave the other as they are equally insecure and afraid of being alone.

Matching or compatible continuum of self values (CSVs) can be categorized into three relationship groups.

- **Normal or healthy**
  A matching positive and negative zero, one or two CSV.

- **Problematic**
  A matching positive and negative three CSV.

- **Unhealthy or dysfunctional**
  A matching positive and negative four or five CSV.

Unhealthy and problematic self-orientations range from (-5 & +5) to (-3 & +3), respectively. Although these CSV pairings or relationships constitute a "balanced" relationship, the inequity of LRC given and taken typically leads to a breakdown in the quality of the relationship. Because the (+3) to (+5)

---

[7] Displays the traits of codependency.

self-oriented individuals all demonstrate narcissistic tendencies, the (-3) to (-5) "others" partner will always be on the "shorter end of the receiving stick." The others-oriented partner typically suffers more than the self-centered or narcissistic partner, as they are denied fair and equitable amounts of LRC. In an effort to avoid upsetting their self-absorbed or self-centered partner, the others-oriented person tends to tolerate and consequently adapt to their partner's narcissistic ways. Because the others partner is neither adept nor comfortable in communicating anger, displeasure or resentment, he is likely to suppress these feelings. To communicate resentment or anger would likely result in rejection, conflict and/or personal or relational harm. By repressing their anger and bitterness, and by placating their narcissistic partner, the others-oriented partner perpetuates the balanced, but dysfunctional relationship.

Individuals with unhealthy and problematic self-orientations are rigidly locked into their dysfunctional self-orientation. Codependents (-5 CSV) and emotional manipulators (+5 CSV), especially, are rigidly inflexible in their self-orientations. Although relationships with a (-4) and (+4) CSV pairing constitute a dysfunctional relationship, both individuals have some capacity, albeit very minimal, to break free of their rigid others-oriented approach to their relationships. To illustrate, the (-4) others-oriented person has some, although very minimal, capacity to set boundaries and seek some level of LRC fulfillment. Likewise, the (+4) self-oriented partner has some, but minimal, capabilities to demonstrate an authentic concern for their partner's LRC needs.

Unhealthy or dysfunctional romantic partnerships are typically incapable of improved relational health, vis-a-vis their rigid and inflexible extreme self-orientations. These relationships resist change mostly because the emotional manipulator's inability to acknowledge their role in the relationship's problems, while also being resistant to seeking help for them. The (-5) codependent is correspondingly resistant to change, as it would result in potential emotional, psychological and even physical harm while also risking the long-term viability of the relationship. Examples include a (+5) emotional manipulator partner, who is unable and unwilling to understand, admit to, or seek help for their destructive role in their relationships. The (-5) codependent could be a severely enabling wife who has threatened to leave her alcoholic husband for 30 years, but never followed through.

The (-4) and (+4) matched CSV relationship is similarly resistant to change. The difference between the 5 and the 4 matched CSV relationships is that the former is less likely to seek and be successful in psychotherapy than the latter. Nevertheless, couples therapy with unhealthy or dysfunctional individuals is often very challenging, as (+5) and (+4) narcissistic individuals are resistant to taking responsibility for their problems while the (-5) and (-4) partners are not inclined to challenge their spouse.

According to the societal and cultural standards of most developed western countries, the (-3) and (+3) relationship is often considered problematic, in that the distribution of LRC is not equally and fairly distributed. In this "problematic" relationship category, the LRC balance is significantly tilted toward the others-oriented individual. Even with the inequity of LRC given and received, this couple is still capable of minor levels of mutuality and reciprocity. For example, the others-oriented partner is able to set some boundaries as well as communicating some of their LRC needs. Conversely, the self-oriented partner is capable of minimal to moderate levels of empathy and motivation to meet their partner's LRC needs, while also being open to some constructive and critical feedback.

The delineation between healthy and unhealthy CSV pairings is not always clear. From the vantage point of modern western culture, a couple with a (-3) and (+3) CSV pairing may be considered unhealthy, as there is a distinct disparity with the exchange of LRC. However, from the perspective of other societies, cultures or ethnic groups in which the norm is oriented toward an acceptable discrepancy between the giving and taking of LRC, then the relationship would be considered healthy. It is likely that individuals outside modern western cultures would deem this relationship as unhealthy or dysfunctional. However, if these romantic partners are satisfied and happy with their relationship and there is no harm perpetrated against the "others" self-oriented individual, then their somewhat polarized self-orientations may actually constitute a culturally specific healthy relationship.

The normal, or healthy, values are (-2), (-1), (0), (+1) and (+2). A person whose self-orientation falls within this range exemplifies a healthy balance of LRC for others and self. Although a (-2) "others" self-oriented person and a (+2) "self" self-oriented person may not share an equal distribution of LRC given and taken, they can experience a healthy and mutually satisfying relationship around their unique self-orientation configuration. This negative and positive CSV pairing is considered a healthy relationship when both partners are content and satisfied with the uneven distribution of LRC given and received. The (-2)/(+2) relationship especially works when both partners feel loved, respected and cared for in a manner that meets their healthy emotional needs.

A healthy relationship, therefore, is not defined by a sum zero balance, but rather by the balance between give and take in a relationship, as represented by mildly opposite self-orientations. However, the sum zero balance is necessary to create a foundation for a healthy equal relationship in which each partner feels that they are giving and receiving the amount of LRC that corresponds to their inversely matching healthy self-orientations.

Except for the emotional manipulator who has a personality disorder, a person's self-orientation or CSV is neither fixed nor permanent.[8] A person's CSV typically ebbs and flows throughout a lifetime. It is possible, albeit not typical, for a person to move from one side of the continuum to another. In the case of a self-orientation switch, the person usually begins with a lower negative or lower positive CSV. This is where psychotherapy is so very crucial to one's mental health. With motivation, emotional fortitude and good psychotherapy, both self- and others self-oriented individuals are able to change their unhealthy self-orientation. It should be noted that because of the psychological constitutional differences between the others and self self-orientations (which is discussed in chapter 8 and 9), the others-oriented individual is more likely to switch self-orientations.

A few possible explanations for one's CSV fluctuations or self-orientation switch could include: normal developmental or maturation processes, religious or spiritual experiences, psychological or mental health services, change of life experiences, age-related transitions, e.g. a midlife experience. It will suffice to say we are not indelibly stamped with a specific personality type or characteristics. Freewill and the motivation to become a better version of one's self fuels emotional growth and psychological healing. It is this author's deep conviction that the human spirit and the human psyche are defined by possibilities and potentialities.

Romantic relationships become healthier when the equal inverse CSVs move closer to zero on the continuum. With the less severe matching CSV's, the relationship is defined more by equality, reciprocity and mutuality. This healthier couple will no longer be polarized by their self-orientation differences. Instead, they will experience a more equal distribution of LRC which will, in turn, create higher levels of harmony and intimacy.

If one partner's CSV moves in a healthier direction (closer to zero) and the other doesn't follow, then the relationship is likely to be in jeopardy. This is common when one partner participates in a mental health or addiction-related service while the other partner does not – ignoring his contribution to the dysfunctional relationship. Relationships with unbalanced CSVs are inherently unstable and subsequently prone to conflict, discord and a break-up.

---

[8] As discussed later in the book, individuals with an emotional manipulator personality disorder are capable of psychological growth. However, the probability for such is very low.

Relationship instability that is caused by increased mental health will occur when a (-5) codependent woman, who is married to the (+5) emotional manipulator man, seeks psychotherapy for her codependency. As a result of progress in therapy, it is likely that her self-orientation/CSV would change for the better, moving closer to zero. Provided her mental health improves and she chooses to remain with her emotional manipulator husband, the relationship will consequently become unstable. Without the zero sum balance, "all bets are off." Conflict and irreconcilable differences are likely to result, as the former codependent will be compelled to seek greater levels of LRC from her husband, which he is not capable of giving her. Even with greater mental health, the formerly codependent client, will experience compelling conscious and unconscious desires to return to former dysfunctional personal and relational levels. Through the continuation and maintenance of her mental health, the zero sum balance will be lost, which will likely result in the end or break-up of the relationship.

It should be noted that stabilization/destabilization concepts are directly influenced by family systems theory, which proposes that individuals cannot be understood in isolation, but rather as a part of a larger relationship or family who together function as one interdependent emotional unit.

Exceptions to the Rule

There are exceptions to the continuum of self theory/the zero sum relationship hypotheses. For example, a romantic couple that does not share a zero sum relationship may be "stable" and resist breaking up for a variety of extenuating reasons, which could include shared financial dependency, medical or insurance needs, or cultural, ethnic or religious requirements. One of many examples includes an arranged marriage, which is customary in some Asian, African and Middle Eastern cultures. Relationship partners of an arranged marriage may experience a healthy and loving relationship directly as a result of their shared values, beliefs and practices. The non-zero-balanced arranged marriage will likely persevere because of the couple's shared respect and agreement for the culturally defined institution of marriage. This couple will also maintain an enduring relationship as a result of strong platonic feelings for each other and shared commitment to their faith and family. However, if their CSVs are not inversely balanced, they will likely never be close, intimate lovers.

Conversely, if this CSV-imbalanced arranged marital couple experiences conflict and is unable to resolve it satisfactorily, and one or both partners experience culturally unacceptable harm, then this culturally normative relationship configuration may be considered unhealthy and dysfunctional.[9]

A person's CSV is not a permanent representation of their relational and mental health. The vast majority of us are capable of overcoming our personal and relationship problems and limitations – becoming healthier individuals. We all, however, experience periods in our lives in which we struggle and move a few steps backwards. As much as we can move backwards, so can we move forward.

The following vignettes illustrate both a healthy and dysfunctional zero sum relationship.

A Healthy Zero Sum Relationship: Susan (-2) and Zach (+2)

Susan is an emotionally/psychologically healthy and balanced person who is mildly others-oriented, as exemplified by her CSV of -2. Susan experiences great joy and fulfillment through her charitable and giving approach to life. She loves organizing parties for others, helping friends decorate their homes, babysitting her sister's children, or simply being a compassionate listener who is always there to provide an ear to listen or a shoulder on which to cry. More than anything, Susan takes great pride in the manner in which she parents her two daughters. She loves cooking their favorite meals, being a Girl Scouts leader, taking them roller-skating and helping them with school projects or homework. Susan is also a part-time office manager for a law firm that requires her to coordinate her high-powered, successful but disorganized, boss's schedule.

Susan is married to Zach, a talented physician whose ambition is to become the chief orthopedic surgeon of the hospital where he works. Although Zach is very busy and often consumed with his professional obligations, he makes time to meet his children's and wife's personal and emotional needs. Even in his reduced capacity, his family feels that they get enough of Zach's attention and love. While the marriage and family life in combination are challenging, and just plain difficult at times, Susan and Zach are jointly committed to making a future together. Susan is very supportive of Zach's professional ambitions, as she and Zach share the same personal, family and career goals and ambitions. Both feel supported by the other while vicariously enjoying each other's accomplishments.

As a supportive wife, Susan is patient with the demands and rigors of Zach's work schedule. Even if it is between his numerous professional obligations or late at night, Susan almost always finds a sympathetic ear when she complains to Zach about having the lion's share of the household

---

[9] It is beyond the scope of this book and this author's experience and knowledge base to further delineate healthy versus dysfunctional levels for individuals who are not a part of the American culture.

and child-rearing duties. What makes Susan healthy and not codependent (CSV of -2 versus a -5), is that she derives a great deal of pleasure and meaning from helping others and, when necessary, is not shy about reaching out for help and support herself.

Even though Susan appreciates and identifies with her giving nature, she is able to set boundaries with others and is able to stand up for what she needs. For example, when she is overwhelmed with work and/or family responsibilities, she is quite capable of gently saying no to a request for her help. Although she doesn't expect the "give and take ratio" to be equal, she knows her limits and has a good internal barometer that directs her toward self-care. All in all, Susan is a healthy and balanced person whose self-orientation slants mildly to moderately towards the needs of others.

Zach is similarly a healthy and balanced person, even with his mild self-orientation (CSV of +2). Zach clearly enjoys his pursuit of professional success. He believes he is doing his part in the marriage and the family by working as hard as he does. Zach (and Susan) believes that his career ambitions are going to result in greater overall comfort and happiness for the family. Although he isn't always happy that he is away from home as much as he is, he knows his professional successes will benefit the people he loves the most: Susan and his children. Even in Zach's diminished personal and familial capacity, he does not hesitate to make Susan feel loved, respected and cared for. When he is unable to be there for an important family event because of an important professional obligation, the family supports him, even though they are disappointed. This relationship works because Zach and Susan's zero sum relationship is balanced and mutually satisfying.

A Dysfunctional Zero Sum Relationship: Sandra (-5) and Paul (+5)

Sandra is a 39-year old beautiful, but obese, woman who is the mother of a special needs child and wife to a man who has all the primary symptoms of a narcissistic personality disorder. She is an emotional eater, self-medicating her sadness, loneliness and anger with food. Sandra is musically gifted. She writes her own music, has an angelic singing voice, plays guitar masterfully and works for her church as the choir and teen worship service director. Despite her musical talent, her standing in the church and her generous nature, Sandra has only received two salary increases during her 15 years of employment. She is considerably underpaid compared to others in her field. The church's congregants adore her and she has become an icon for all those who have been taught by her.

Despite Sandra's flawless record, Reverend Doeman, the leader of the church, and the board of directors have historically neglected to give her well-deserved pay raises and promotions. She has not asked for a raise, naïvely believing that if she deserves one, it will be offered to her. Recently, Reverend Doeman demoted her to assistant music director and hired a long-time friend to take on the newly created associate pastor position, which would absorb her choir and teen director responsibilities. Sandra was humiliated by this and, to add insult to injury, she heard about it from another staff member. When Sandra shared her feelings with the Reverend, as in the past when he was confronted about any wrong-doing, he became quietly angry, defensive and manipulatively cast himself as the victim who can never make everyone happy. All the while defending himself, he would complement Sandra's competency and implore her to not be upset with him. Instead of standing her ground and confronting Reverend Doeman's excuses and rationalizations, she apologized for upsetting him. Because Sandra feels powerless and is fearful and avoidant of conflict, she stuffs or suppresses her anger and resentment toward the church, especially Reverend Doeman.

Sandra's son is a lovable and sweet young man, but has the misfortune of being diagnosed with multiple psychiatric disorders, generalized anxiety disorder and attention deficit hyperactivity disorder (ADHD). In addition to his psychiatric challenges, he has extremely low self-esteem and problematic social and academic functioning. Sandra has never been consistent at setting limits with most people, especially her family members. Consequently, her son rarely listens to her requests and refuses to help her with household chores. Because of feeling bad for her son's mental health and social problems, she refrains from punishing him when he misbehaves.

Sandra met her husband Paul when they were both 18-year-old freshmen in college. Despite nagging doubts about Paul's self-centeredness, selfishness and immaturity, she fell deeply in love with him. Sandra was extremely attracted to Paul because he, like her, enjoyed the raw excitement of their sexual relationship. Sandra was completely enamored with Paul's playful, spontaneous, and rebellious personality. She even liked his arrogant but charming "edge."

During their junior year, Sandra and Paul spontaneously decided to get married. Although she had wanted to wait, Paul convinced her that by getting married, he would be more motivated in college and would consequently be more successful in his future career. Although she had many concerns about marrying Paul, she was convinced that no other man would be interested in marrying her because of her obesity and her insecurities. Sandra's desperation to get married and have children nullified any moments of intuition that Paul was not a suitable lifelong partner.

Sandra was genuinely confused about how she felt about marrying Paul. Her alcoholic father and severely dependent and insecure mother had been poor role models for healthy love. Without experience with healthy and mutually loving relationships, Sandra sincerely believed her love for Paul was realistic and healthy. Shortly after their nuptials, Paul dropped out of college, as he was failing most of his classes. Sandra did not know about Paul's failing grades, as he kept it secret from her. Paul blamed his academic failures on his professors, who he was convinced had personal vendettas against him. What Paul failed to understand was that his poor academic performance combined with his arrogant and disrespectful treatment of his teachers, earned him a reputation among his professors as being a problem student. Because Paul's college was unsympathetic to his request for academic probation, he dropped out of college.

After quitting college, Paul slipped into a state of depression and was consequently unmotivated to do most anything except drink a lot of beer and smoke plenty of marijuana. As a result of Sandra's constant requests for him to get a job and to contribute to their finances, Paul reluctantly found a job at an auto dealership where he made a dollar over minimum wage cleaning the used car inventory. As a result of Paul's lack of motivation to contribute emotionally and financially, their marriage quickly became stressful. One year into their marriage, Sandra became pregnant with what would be her only child. Paul was uninterested in Sandra's pregnancy and seemed to distance himself further away from her. Two months after their son Tyler was born, Sandra discovered Paul was having an affair with one of his co-workers. Sandra did not dare to confront Paul as she was terrified of being left behind for another woman. Because of Sandra's terribly low self-esteem and her self-loathing, she sincerely believed no other man would ever find her appealing or worthy of a long-term romantic relationship.

Paul was rarely personally and emotionally engaged with Sandra and his child. Paul preferred his guy friends at his vintage auto club, where he always had an audience for his immature charm, his tall tales, jokes and drinking binges. Sandra gave up on confronting Paul, as it never resulted in any long-term change. She also stopped confronting Paul about his wrongdoings, as his temper flare-ups became progressively more threatening and frightening. Sandra simply quit believing that he would ever listen to her requests and pleas. Sandra had grown accustomed to feeling invisible and unappreciated in and outside of her marriage.

When Sandra did confront Paul about his infidelity, she often fell victim to his tearful emotional promises to change (stopping his lying and infidelity) and his pleas for her to not leave him. Eventually, Sandra became numb to the pain that Paul caused her and consequently stopped expecting him to contribute to the family in any way except for a paycheck and medical insurance. Paul's habitual deception and infidelity shattered any hopes Sandra had of being loved, respected and cared for.

Paul's career never progressed past the same position at the auto dealership from when they were first married. Twenty very unhappy years later, Paul has remained unchanged; he has just been caught in his fifth affair. Over the years, he was absent as a lover, confidant, partner and father. Likewise, Sandra's insecurities, poor self-esteem and fear of confronting Paul remain unchanged, as her insecurities and confusion about her marriage kept her tied to a narcissistic, selfish and dishonest husband.

Sandra is loyal and helpful to everyone in her life, always available to lend a hand when needed. Known as the "go-to" person in her community, she provides assistance to others who are in need of her nurturing and patient support. While wanting to say no to the multiple requests for her time and energy, she is unable to set boundaries, and feels guilty when she thinks about asking someone else to do something for her. Her happy and upbeat exterior hides a secret cache of anger and shame that no one seems to want to reciprocate the help and love that she demonstrates.

Sandra is a classic (-5) codependent as she puts everyone else's needs in front of her own. She cares tirelessly for her child, husband, friends and people at the church, while receiving little or nothing in return. She has never left her self-centered, emotionally abusive and philandering husband out of fear of being alone and unable to pay the bills. Her obesity unrealistically reinforces her belief that no one could ever love her, and generates feelings of powerlessness to change the nature of her one-sided relationships. Although Sandra fantasizes about standing up to the narcissistic and intimidating people in her life, she ultimately chooses to capitulate to them. Sandra self-medicates her feelings of worthlessness through her eating binges. Since marrying Paul, Sandra's weight has increased by 100 pounds. Even with her doctor's warnings, Sandra seems powerless to change her emotional eating patterns.

Paul is a typical (+5) narcissist. More specifically, Paul would fit the diagnostic criteria for narcissistic personality disorder. Paul's approach to life is almost completely focused around his own personal and emotional needs – at the exclusion and expense of the needs of others, especially his wife and child. He and Sandra are perfectly, if miserably, compatible as their combined CSV create a zero sum relationship. Together, their self-orientations are inversely compatible.

This "perfectly" matched opposite relationship will likely remain stable as Sandra's poor self-esteem and deep feelings of insecurity create feelings of powerlessness about changing the circumstances in her life, such as divorcing Paul. In addition, Sandra, in a distorted manner, maintains the belief that she still loves Paul. Paul wouldn't dream of leaving Sandra, as he has the "perfect" wife who will do everything for him as well as not hold him accountable for his numerous selfish and narcissistic shortcomings. Paul does not want to divorce Sandra as he similarly has a distorted feeling of love and commitment to Sandra. He also wouldn't want to leave her as he relies on Sandra to take care of Tyler and the house, pay the bills, and maintain their social group. This marriage is considered stable as Paul and Sandra are both locked into their relationship and neither is motivated nor psychologically capable of leaving the other.

Two years after Sandra started therapy with me, she lost 75 pounds, divorced Paul, quit her church job, got hired by an employer who empowers her and rewards her contributions, severed the relationships with her narcissistic friends, and created healthier and more mutually satisfying relationships with the rest of her friends and family. Sandra also turned a corner with her son, as she became more confident, consistent and less fearful in her parenting approach. As a result of her strides in psychotherapy, Sandra's CSV changed from a (-5) to a (-2), placing her on the healthy side of the continuum of self. Sandra is now dating Bill, a wonderful man, whose CSV is a (+2). Together, these two are happy and mutually and reciprocally loving, respectful and caring.

Maslow's Hammer and Nail Theory

As much as I attempt to define and quantify human relationship behavior through the use of the continuum of self theory, it is neither feasible nor appropriate to rely on just one theory to explain complicated human behavior patterns. There are inherent dangers to having a limited view on human psychology. According to Abraham Maslow, one of the founders of humanistic psychological theory, "I suppose it is tempting, if the only tool you have is a hammer, to treat everything as if it were a nail." Let this "hammer" be one of many tools in a tool box that we can use to understand and change our dysfunctional relationships.

It should be noted that the continuum of self measures only a person's orientation of self. It does not purport to measure more complicated and multifaceted personality characteristics. The best determination of one's self-orientation comes from the assessment and diagnostic process by a competent and qualified psychotherapist trained in the continuum of self theory.

Because the compatible but opposite self-orientation personality types are just one of many possible personality type categories, it is presumed that other personality traits or constructs may have their own unique attraction process. To illustrate, mentally ill, economically disadvantaged, politically disenfranchised, physically challenged, and other impaired, challenged or oppressed groups of individuals may have their own unique relationship attraction dynamics.

Although the continuum of self theory attempts to explain and simplify the complicated and multi-faceted attraction dynamic, it does not pretend to be bigger and more inclusive than it was designed to be. It is a narrowly focused explanatory paradigm that measures an individual's self-orientation while accounting for the attraction dynamic of opposite but compatible personality types. It is not intended to be a stand-alone or comprehensive theoretical explanation. It may be useful as an adjunct to other psychological theories.

The author believes the continuum of self theory is both a valid and reliable psychological construct. However, as a new psychological theory, it has not yet met the rigors of scientific scrutiny. It is my hope that the continuum of self theory and the other concepts presented broaden our current understanding of human behavior, as well as stimulate further thought and discussion.

CHAPTER 6
The Emotional Manipulation Disorders – Defining the Disorder

The terms, "emotional manipulator" or "emotional manipulation disorders" are relatively new to the mental health field. Because it is not yet a commonly recognized mental health or clinical disorder, the term has not yet taken on a universally accepted definition. If taken at face value, an emotional manipulator is someone who manipulates the emotions of others. For the purposes of this book and my seminars, the term "emotional manipulation disorders" is used as a specific category of psychological disorders. An emotional manipulator is someone who is diagnosed with narcissistic, borderline or antisocial personality disorder. An emotional manipulator is also a person who is addicted to drugs/alcohol or a behavior/process, whose addiction has driven them to behave narcissistically and harmfully in their relationships. Although the three personality disorders and an addiction disorder are demonstrably different from each other, all four share similar narcissistic personality traits.

Narcissistic personality disorder, the first subtype, describes a person who has an inflated sense of superiority and importance while being preoccupied with thoughts and feelings of success and power. The second subtype, borderline personality disorder, loves others with great intensity and passion. However, if they perceive the possibility of judgment, disapproval, criticism or abandonment, they will often strike back with a fury of hateful and vindictive aggression. The third, antisocial personality disorder, describes an individual who is deceitful, cunning, covertly manipulative and purposefully exploitative. The last subtype, an addiction disorder, describes an addict who, because of his addiction, behaves in a dishonest, manipulative, selfish, and self-centered manner. Addicts are typically physically and psychologically dependent on a substance or mood-altering behavior pattern, e.g., sex, gambling, spending.

Almost anyone can create a term describing a psychological condition, a psychiatric disorder or a behavioral affliction. These terms, when widely accepted, have inherent power to help or even save lives. Or they can be misused to stereotype, generalize, harm or even destroy the lives or livelihood of others. It is crucial that we honor and respect the impact and power that these descriptive labels or diagnoses carry. It is very important for clinicians, behavioral health researchers and writers to research and validate new diagnostic terms, such as the ones used in this book, e.g., "emotional manipulation disorder." Therefore, if the terms or diagnostic labels outlined in this book are to be used by either the general public or by mental health or medical practitioners, it is imperative that universally accepted definitions be created.

For the purposes of this book, an operational definition for the term "emotional manipulator" has been created. Instead of being an arbitrary or subjective description, the definition is specific and accounts for its multiple dimensions. This new definition attempts to standardize the term, while specifically describing both its qualitative and quantitative aspects. In other words, the newly created definition for "emotional manipulator" and "emotional manipulation disorders" utilizes descriptive language that illustrates and specifies inherent characteristics, while also assigning a system of measurement to it, e.g., the continuum of self values (CSV).

The emotional manipulation disorders cannot be understood without an understanding of how they manifest within a relationship. It follows the logic that if you were going to understand the problems of alcoholism, it would be necessary to understand the alcoholic's relationship with their partner – the co-alcoholic or codependent. As much as the definition of alcoholism or, for that matter, chemical dependency requires a descriptive account of its psychological and physiological characteristics, the definition would be incomplete without information regarding its relational components. After all, it is common knowledge that the alcoholic's partner is inexorably connected to both the problem and the treatment. To that end, it is imperative to understand the emotional manipulator's relationships with others, principally the codependent partner. Emotional manipulators and codependents go "hand in hand" as they both are magnetically and inescapably attracted to each other. Neither could demonstrate their psychopathological personality traits without the other. To understand what an emotional manipulation disorder is, it is impossible not to learn about the emotional manipulator/codependent relationship.

According to the continuum of self theory, emotional manipulators have a *self-orientation* that is almost completely focused on their own needs and desires at the exclusion of the needs and desires of their significant others. Not only do they require a disproportionate amount of love, respect and care from their partners, they are unable and unwilling to reciprocate. When they do demonstrate positive regard, affection or generosity, strings are usually attached.

When "plotted" on the continuum of self, they have the most "severe" CSV: a (+5). Individuals with severe "positive" CSVs are unable to unconditionally demonstrate love, respect and care for others and are typically unaware of how their narcissism and selfishness hurts those who they claim to love. *It should be noted that all of the emotional manipulator disorders are distinctly narcissistic in nature.*

Personality Disorders

A definition of a personality disorder and an addiction disorder will help the reader to better understand the emotional manipulation disorders. According to the DSM-IV-TR™ (Diagnostic and Statistical Manual of Mental Disorders Version IV – Text Revision), personality disorders are a class of personality types and enduring behavioral patterns associated with significant distress or disability, which appear to deviate from social and cultural expectations, particularly in relating to other people. To qualify for this diagnosis, the individual, because of their personality disorder, has to be impaired socially, occupationally or in other important areas of functioning.

At present, there are ten personality disorders listed in the DSM. Inherent in all personality disorders are deeply ingrained maladaptive patterns of behavior, emotions and thinking, which may be identified as early as adolescence and often persist for a lifetime. It is a widely accepted practice, as well as a DSM requirement, that most personality disorders are not formerly diagnosed until the age of 18. Since these disorders are considered permanent in nature, it is incumbent on diagnosticians/ clinicians to respect the impact of including this diagnosis in someone's mental health or medical records. Thanks to our current insurance system, certain mental health diagnoses are used to exclude an individual from affordable insurance, or even from being insured.

Personality disordered individuals have difficulty controlling their impulses and moderating their pathological behavior. They also have difficulties expressing socially appropriate emotions, relating to others and forming and maintaining reciprocal and mutually satisfying relationships. They are oblivious to their psychological deficits, eccentric conduct and dysfunctional perceptual and thought patterns. Without an ability to accurately perceive, comprehend and, consequently, adapt to the accepted forms of personal and social behaviors, they experience significant problems and limitations in their social encounters and in most of their significant relationships, i.e., work, family and personal relationships. Not possessing insight into their psychological deficits and the resulting harm they cause others, they typically blame others or project their problems and inadequacies onto other people.[10] Without an accurate and subjective understanding of their limitations and psychopathology, as well as their negative impact on others, they typically do not seek psychotherapeutic services.

Personality disordered individuals simply do not think they have a problem. Especially individuals with one of the emotional manipulator personality disorders will not admit to having a problem(s) or causing harm or grief to another person, as to do so would run contrary to their narcissistic personality make-up (grandiosity, entitlement, vanity, etc.). If they do admit to a problem or to an element of their personality that is problematic, it is usually because they were caught red-handed in a lie or they are trying to manipulate their way out of being held accountable for a hurtful act.

Individuals who are addicted to a drug or a particular behavior, such as sex or gambling, qualify for the emotional manipulator diagnosis only if, in addition, they demonstrate the significant pathological traits of any of the three emotional manipulator personality disorders. The difference, however, is that the addiction, not an underlying psychological disturbance, is responsible for their psychopathological or dysfunctional behavior. In other words, the addiction itself compels them to behave similarly to any of the three emotional manipulation personality disorders. For example, they may be self-centered and egotistic like the narcissist, erratic, reactive and harmful to those they love like the borderline, or dishonest and manipulative like the antisocial personality disordered individual.

An addiction disorder is a catchall phrase for the persistent and compulsive dependence on a habit-forming substance or behavior. Despite negative consequences, individuals with addiction disorders are compelled to continue the use of a specific mood-altering substance or to continue a destructive and repetitive behavioral pattern. This is a progressive disorder that has its origins in the brain. Or, as Alcoholics Anonymous refers to it − a disease. Over time, addicts increase the frequency and amount of their drug or addictive behavior of choice in order to achieve the "normal" euphoric or "high" experience. With regular use, increased tolerance for the drug or euphoria causing the behavior is developed. Tolerance is the process by which the addict requires

---

[10] Projection is a defense mechanism whereby a person unconsciously <u>denies</u> his or her own undesirable attributes, thoughts and emotions, which are then ascribed to the outside world, usually to other people. It is the "spot it you got it" defense mechanism.

increasingly larger amounts of the addictive substance/behavior to achieve the original euphoric effects and eventually even to feel normal.

Physical dependency eventually occurs as result of the continued and progressively increased drug/behavior "usage." Physical dependency on the drug/behavior compels addicts to maintain their usage patterns while progressively increasing the frequency and amounts of their drug of choice. If they should radically decrease or terminate their drug or addictive behavior patterns, the addict will likely experience a withdrawal syndrome (symptoms). Withdrawal symptoms include, but are not limited to, anxiety, irritability, intense cravings for the substance, nausea, hallucinations, headaches, cold sweats and tremors. Even after the withdrawal symptoms subside, the addict often experiences an irrational desire to return to their destructive and often life-threatening drug abuse or behaviors. For this reason, an addiction is often considered a life-long affliction.

CHAPTER 7

The Human Magnet Syndrome

When it comes to romantic relationships, we are all human magnets! *The Human Magnet Syndrome* is another metaphorical explanation of the unconscious force that brings opposite, but compatible, companions together into an enduring and stable relationship. Although much simpler and less comprehensive than the continuum of self theory, it follows the same basic tenet that two prospective romantic partners are attracted to each other as a result of their opposite, but well-matched, and compatible personality types. While the continuum of self focuses on a person's self-orientation or continuum of self value (CSV), the Human Magnet Syndrome conceptualizes the attraction dynamic through the use of a metaphorical compass and magnets, which, like the real things, operate by the properties of magnetism. As human magnets, we are pulled toward a particular romantic partner whose "magnetic polarity" is opposite to ours.

Despite our efforts to find a romantic partner who unconditionally loves, respects and cares for us and who participates in a mutual and reciprocal relationship, we are inclined to follow a metaphorical "love compass" that will powerfully direct our relationship choices. Whether we realize it or not, we all use a metaphorical compass when we seek an ideal romantic partner. We are obliged to follow the direction in which we are led, regardless of our conscious intentions to take a different route. Even with our promises to ourselves to make rational, safe and healthy choices, we are unable to resist the captivating pull toward the direction that our compass points. Star-crossed lovers, therefore, are inevitably brought together not because of their conscious choices, but rather because their metaphorical compass has directed them into each other's loving embrace.

The romantic relationship that is brought together by an interminably strong magnetic force will survive the test of time, as it adheres to the human instinct to find and stay with a partner who is uniquely compatible and familiar. According to the continuum of self theory, compatible romantic partners tend to stay true to their unique opposite relationship orientation. The same applies to the human magnet syndrome: We are attracted to and maintain relationships with individuals whose "magnetic polarity" is uniquely opposite and therefore compatible with our own.

Positive and Negative Magnetic Forces

As human magnets, we all possess either a positive or negative magnetic charge that naturally compels us to be attracted to a person with an opposite magnetic charge. While the continuum of self theory refers to matching inverse personality types as self-orientations, the Human Magnet Syndrome refers to them as positive or negative *magnetic roles.* The term magnetic role was intentionally chosen for its metaphoric equivalent to the positive or negative magnetic pole of metal magnets. Codependency or the (-5) CSV is metaphorically equivalent to a **negative** magnetic role or negative human magnet charge. The emotional manipulator disorder or the (+5) CSV is metaphorically equivalent to a **positive** magnetic role or positive human magnet charge.

As human magnets, we all have a specific metaphorical magnetic charge that is attracted to another person's opposite, but matching magnetic charge. Similar to the continuum of self theory, the human magnet syndrome is largely an unconscious process. Notwithstanding, romantic allure and relationship "chemistry" is also directed by palpable conscious processes. While we find ourselves unconsciously moving in the direction of a romantic partner's unique personal magnetism, we are also highly influenced by what we see, think, and perceive.

Just like metal magnets which form a magnetic bond when two opposite poles come into contact, human magnets are brought together by their opposite but matching magnetic roles (aka self-orientations). The person who is oriented toward the needs of others carries a negative charge. The person who is oriented toward their own needs will carry a positive charge. Just as in the continuum of self theory, two uniquely opposite but compatible romantic partners will irresistibly be pulled toward each other, not so much by their conscious decisions or intentions, but rather by the interaction of their opposite magnetic fields. Partners with complementary magnetic roles are irresistibly drawn together and locked into a relationship that is nearly impossible to resist or break free of. The powerful "magnetic" pull toward each other results in an irresistible and enduring romantic relationship. Whether healthy or dysfunctional, the two "human magnets" are amorously controlled by the nature of their own relationship magnetism.

As the north pole of a metal magnet is always attracted to the south pole of another magnet, so will individuals with a positive magnetic role be attracted to individuals with a negative magnetic role. The attraction properties are associated with a corresponding continuum of self value (CSV). Magnetic roles, like CSVs, are inversely and proportionally attracted to each other. To illustrate, a person with a severe others self-orientation, a codependent, has a CSV of (-5). The strongest negative magnet role charge and a (-5) CSV are analogously equivalent measurements of the same personality type. Conversely, a person with a severe self-orientation toward their needs only, an emotional manipulator, will have a CSV of (+5). The strongest positive magnet role charge and the (+5) CSV are equivalent. Simply stated, negatively-charged magnet roles, or negative CSVs, are always attracted to positively-charged magnet roles, or positive CSVs. The relationship dance between a codependent and an emotional manipulator and the magnetic attraction of the codependent and the emotional manipulator are metaphorical explanations for the same process.

As much as individuals with negative magnet roles are always attracted to individuals with positive magnetic roles, similar magnetic roles will always repel each other. Individuals with similar magnetic roles will experience a formidable force of magnetic repulsion, making it nearly impossible to connect romantically. This parallels the continuum of self theory's explanation of the repulsion of like self-orientations. Two emotional manipulators or two codependents will almost always create anti-romantic chemistry. They will find each other uninteresting and feel a distinct sense of repulsion. This is why, when we meet a person that might seem perfect "on paper," there might be no spark...no romantic chemistry. This is what we feel when we hug or kiss a prospective romantic interest, who despite our hopes, seems more like a friend than a lover.

To illustrate the power of the Human Magnet Syndrome with healthy romantic partners, my brother and sister-in-law, David and Erika, gave me permission to include their love at first sight story. David, a 21-year old U.S. Army soldier, and Erika, a 24-year old Chilean visiting the USA on a student Visa, frequented the same community pool in Arlington, Virginia. At the time, *neither David nor Erika spoke the other's language.* When Erika and David first laid eyes on each other, they experienced an electric-like charge of magnetic attraction. David recalled thinking that Erika was the most beautiful women he had ever seen. Erika was similarly instantly and completely drawn to David's good looks and charm. For both of them, it was love at first sight – a feeling that, up until that time, neither had ever experienced. Neither could have guessed that this would happen with a person whose language and culture was completely different from their own.

It took several weeks before David and Erika had the courage to start their first conversation, which naturally would be a challenge because neither spoke the other's language. Their initial conversations took the form of three to four word questions and answers. Even with this problem, neither could resist the intense and uncontrollable impulse to get closer to each other. David recounted that, in the beginning, he would miss a night's sleep just thinking about being with Erika. From the moment David laid eyes on Erika, he experienced a flood of intense emotional and physical sensation. Erika recalled a similar explosive emotional experience.

David and Erika fondly recalled their first night together when they just gazed into each other's eyes and rubbed noses together, feeling no need to speak a word or be more physically intimate. For both, time stood still as they were swept away into a place of emotional ecstasy. Up until that time, neither had experienced such intense and euphoric feelings of emotional attraction.

Determined to communicate, they relied on the resources that were at their immediate disposal. David communicated to Erika through notes, which she would take to her English teacher to translate. Erika would answer these notes and ask David questions through one of David's Army friends who spoke both English and Spanish fluently. Although Erika and David struggled with not speaking each other's language, as healthy human magnets neither would let it get in the way of their intense and compelling feelings of attraction. In actuality, the language of love, or the power of the human magnet syndrome, superseded their struggles with their spoken language and stark cultural differences.

Within three months of their first encounter, both David and Erika began to communicate in each other's language. The irresistible magnetic force that brought them together would culminate in marriage five months after they met. Twenty-two years later, this bond keeps them connected, despite the ups and downs that are normal in all healthy relationships. Language and culture were no match for the human magnet syndrome!

Complimentary Attraction

As complimentary explanations, the human magnet syndrome and the continuum of self theory similarly account for the reflexive and seemingly automatic attraction experience between individuals with dissimilar but well matched personalities. While the Human Magnet analogy is more basic and one-dimensional, both view the relationship attraction dynamics as being driven by opposite but dually reciprocating forces. The Human Magnet analogy differs in that it attributes to the fascination and allure of another person as emanating from a powerful magnetic-like love force. This love force pulls together two distinctly opposite individuals who for all practical purposes seem incompatible, but who really are very well-matched lovers. This force brings together happy and healthy prospective romantic partners as well as those who are considered unhealthy or dysfunctional, e.g. codependents and emotional manipulators.

The magnet-like enticement is formidable and virtually impossible to resist. It is unyielding as it defies conscious attempts to modify or control it. Regardless of the promises made to one's self or others to not repeat past relationship mistakes, a seemingly automatic and predetermined magnetically guided pattern is followed. Despite warning flags or obvious signs of danger, it is nearly impossible to break the magnetic lock of perfectly compatible magnetic roles, be they healthy or dysfunctional. The human magnet syndrome is ultimately responsible for bringing together two outwardly different but highly compatible individuals into an enduring and dysfunctionally resilient relationship. Its power over us is undeniable.

The magnet-like force that brings two opposite but compatible romantic couples together also has the capacity to coerce them into staying in their relationship, despite being unhappy, unsatisfied or hurt. This attraction force is powerful enough to undermine our deeply held personal convictions, values and morals, even overshadowing the customs and social traditions that have been indoctrinated by our family, culture, religion or society. As much as we might try to withstand the alluring power of the human magnet syndrome, many of us fall prey to its ubiquitously seductive and controlling nature.

When Two Human Magnets Meet

The following Internet dating story exemplifies what happens when two outwardly attracted individuals meet and despite their common interests, find out that their "magnets" repel each other.

Jason, my client, and Sally found each other on a popular Internet dating site. This particular site utilizes a patented computer algorithm that helps registered users find individuals who share similar interests and who are uniquely compatible. When Jason and Sally started to correspond, they knew they were a great match because they had virtually the same interests in politics, recreation, religion, music and movies. Based on the pictures that were posted, they were both sure that they were also physically compatible. Their emails were exciting and full of interesting and stimulating conversations. After a week of email messages, they began talking on the phone. These conversations were always lively and engaging. They typically spent over an hour at a time talking to each other. Their first call lasted four hours! Convinced that they were a good match, they decided to set up a date and meet for dinner.

Jason was very excited to meet Sally. In fact, he didn't sleep well the night before their date. When Jason first saw Sally, he recalled thinking she was beautiful, maybe even more so than in her photos. Sally also appreciated Jason's appearance. The first hour of the date went extremely well as they continued their previous conversations, but all the while, Jason kept thinking that the "chemistry" he experienced on email and the phone was just not there. Although he couldn't put his finger on it, he dismissed the thought as being too analytical. The second hour of the date seemed a bit tense as they both seemed to run out of things to say. Jason remembers wanting badly to feel closer to Sally, but it just seemed like something was missing. The date ended with pleasantries and a promise to repeat their dinner experience. With no physical or emotional chemistry, they only shook each other's hands and walked to their respective vehicles.

Unlike in the beginning, Jason did not feel compelled to talk to Sally (email, text or phone call) every day. It took five days before he called her. Because Sally had not called him, he thought the feelings were mutual. When they did talk next, the conversation took on a more muted emotional feel. Being honest, open and communicative people, they openly discussed the slightly uncomfortable "vibe" of their first date. Agreeing that first dates are usually awkward, a second dinner date was planned.

On the second date, as much as Jason and Sally wanted their personal chemistry to work, it did not. Although they still found each other interesting, the romantic allure wasn't there. After dinner, Jason walked Sally to her car and decided to kiss her. He thought a kiss, for sure, would strike up the chemistry that had been missing. As his mouth moved toward hers, Sally moved her face so that his kiss landed on her cheek. She gently pulled away and said what he already knew: There just wasn't any romantic chemistry. Both agreed, laughed and instantly became more relaxed. They decided to keep in touch and try friendship instead.

Ten years later, Jason and Sally are both happily married to individuals who "blew their socks off" when they first met. Jason and Sally have managed to forge a meaningful platonic relationship over the years. This story exemplifies the power of the Human Magnet Syndrome – when two individuals are physically and personally compatible, but not "magnetically matched."

To summarize, the Human Magnet Syndrome is yet another metaphorical explanation for both healthy and dysfunctional relationships. One way or another, we will likely be drawn into a romantic relationship by not so much as what we believe, but more by our "dance preferences," our matching self-orientations and/or by the ubiquitous force of the Human Magnet Syndrome.

CHAPTER 8

For most of our history, children were viewed simply as small versions of adults. Until the late 19th century, the prevailing thoughts on child development were based on the English philosopher, John Locke's (1632-1704), "tabula rasa" explanation. He and his contemporaries believed that the mind of a newborn infant is a "tabula rasa," or blank slate, on which experience writes. It wasn't until the late 19th and early 20th centuries that the psychological and medical sciences began to understand the progressive and sequential developmental psychological stages through which all children pass. In as early as 1915, Sigmund Freud provided the first comprehensive, albeit controversial, theory that connected a person's early childhood experiences, especially with their parent caregiver, with their adult psychological health. Freud theorized that children were motivated by urges to satisfy their biological (including sexual) needs. His theory contains five different psychosexual stages that a child passes through.

Erik Erikson, a renowned developmental psychologist and personality theorist, built upon Freud's developmental theory by emphasizing the role of culture and society and the conflicts that can take place within a person. Erikson created a psychological and social (psychosocial) developmental theory that was based upon eight distinct developmental stages, each with two possible outcomes –success or failure. In each stage, a person experiences unique age-appropriate biological, social and psychological developmental challenges. By successfully completing a particular stage, an individual acquires the psychosocial abilities/skills necessary to move on to the next stage. Progress through a stage is, in part, determined by an individual's success or lack of success in previous stages. When unable to move beyond a specific psychosocial stage, say because of early childhood psychological trauma, the person's future mental health is impacted, if not stunted. George Boeree, a retired professor at Shippensburg University in

Pennsylvania uses a rose metaphor to capture the essence of the Erikson's psychosocial developmental theory:

> **A little like the unfolding of a rose bud, each petal opens up at a certain time, in a certain order, which nature, through its genetics, has determined. If we interfere in the natural order of development by pulling a petal forward prematurely or out of order, we ruin the development of the entire flower.**
>
> (G. Boeree, 2006)

Freud, Erikson and Developmental Psychology

According to Freud, Erikson and almost every other developmental theorist, early childhood experiences are inexorably tied to the development of adult personalities. If all goes well, a child who has experienced safety, emotional nurturance, and love will be adequately prepared for adulthood. The cherished and loved child will likely enter adulthood with positive mental health. However, if a child endures deprivation, neglect or abuse, his future psychological health may not be so promising. Without experiencing protection and adequate nurturing, this child will most likely reach adulthood with distinct psychological and social limitations. Receiving *conditional* love while experiencing neglect, deprivation and/or abuse, will likely culminate in adult psychological or mental health problems. Sadly, for these misfortunate children, the stage will have been set for future dysfunctional adult relationships.

Marsh and Wolfe (2008) explain the predictable nature of child development:

> **Child development follows a predictable, organized course beginning with the child's mastery of physiological regulations (eating, sleeping), and continuing through the development of higher skills, such as problem solving and peer relationships. However, under abnormal and unusual circumstances, especially abuse and neglect, predictability and organization are disrupted and thrown off course, which results in developmental failure and limited adaptation.**
>
> (p. 35)

As much as Freud, Erikson and other developmental psychologists attributed early environmental influences to the development of adult psychological problems, the development of the brain must be also considered. For example, the human brain increases to 80% of the adult weight by the age of four (Prabhakar, 2006). During this 4 year period, a child's formative years, the most rapid physical, cognitive and emotional growth occurs. A child's physical and emotional environment has dramatic impact on the healthy development of their nervous system, primarily their brain. What goes right or wrong during this critical stage of development can affect the child's life thereafter.

Infants are hardwired to be sensitive to, and impacted by, their early environments. Children raised in safe and secure environments by nurturing parents are likely to be psychologically prepared for their future adulthood. Conversely, children raised by parents who were unable or unmotivated to meet their unique psychological and physical needs will be distinctly less successful in adulthood. The child, who is abused, neglected or deprived by one or both of their parents, will sustain emotional harm and possibly psychological damage. These children are forced to adapt to environments that are fraught with risk and danger. Examples of such environments include marital violence, neglect, a parent's alcoholism, and sexual or physical abuse. Raised in harmful and damaging environments, the child's future psychological skills and abilities, e.g., their self-esteem, identity and self-concept, will likely be impaired.

It is a part of human nature for an adult to mimic or repeat significant elements of his own parents' child-rearing style. If we are lucky, our parents would have loved and cared for us in a manner that would have provided us with a stable psychological foundation; and it is likely we would replicate this experience with our own children. If we were not so fortunate and our parents neglected or abused us, it is likely that we would unconsciously be compelled to repeat the "sins" of our own parents on our own children. The saying "you reap what you sow" underscores the impact that parents have on the next generation of mothers and fathers.

According to the renowned American psychologist, Harry Harlow, humans (and most primates) transfer their own child-rearing and parent-bonding experiences to the children they produce (Harlow, 1963). John Bowlby, a British psychologist who is best known for his attachment theory, hypothesized that the parenting style and specific personal mannerisms of human beings, unlike most other species of mammal, are based mostly on learned behavior, not instinct (Bowlby, 1983). Bowlby and Harlow both understood that our parents' dysfunction travels down a generational road to eventually merge lanes with the next generation of children.

Bowlby revolutionized our thinking about the implications of a child's disrupted bond or attachment to a caregiver, which could be a response to bereavement, separation from a parent, deprivation, neglect and abuse. Bowlby hypothesized that an infant's bond or attachment with his caregiver is powerfully correlated with, if not predictive of, his adult attachments or relationships. Hazan and Shaver (1987) expanded upon Bowlby's hypotheses by demonstrating that an infant's attachment experience with his adult caregiver is later replicated in his adult romantic relationships. Through their research, Hazan and Shaver illustrated that adult romantic relationships, like those of infant and caregiver, are deep, emotionally bonded relationships; and are indelibly connected to the early childhood attachment experience. In other words, Hazan and Shaver hypothesized that healthy (non-disrupted) infant-caregiver relationships share similar features with healthy adult-adult romantic relationships. Hazan and Shaver's list exemplifies this connection:

- Both feel safe when the other is nearby and responsive

- Both engage in close, intimate, bodily contact

- Both feel insecure when the other is inaccessible

- Both share discoveries with one another

- Both exhibit a mutual fascination and preoccupation with one another

- Both engage in "baby talk"

Family Dysfunction To The Next Generation

According to most family systems theories, dysfunctional family patterns are passed down from one generation to the next – a transgenerational movement of family dysfunction. Murray Bowen, one of the founders of family systems theory and systemic therapy, believed that it is in the nature of a family that its members are intensely emotionally connected. He postulated that the family unit or system powerfully influences each family member's mental health.

> **"Family members so profoundly affect each other's thoughts, feelings and actions that it often seems as if people are living under the same "emotional skin."**

(www.BowenCenter.org, 2012)

According to Bowen, most families, especially dysfunctional ones, tend to resist change, as change is experienced as stressful and uncomfortable. Bowen explained that when a young adult attempts to become independent from the family they were born in to, or to differentiate from them, they are deeply influenced, if not controlled, by the family's countervailing forces. Change, even if good for the differentiating child, may be perceived as a threat. Hence, some families attempt to preserve their dysfunctional heritage through direct and tacit manipulative strategies. Individuals who did not or were not able to differentiate from their family are more likely to become fused with the predominant family's dysfunctional personality elements. These individuals either conform themselves to others in order to please them, or they attempt to force others to conform to them (Bowen, 1993). Hence, all families, especially dysfunctional ones, not only resist change, but pass down their shared emotional functioning to the next generation.

The transgenerational movement of dysfunctional family patterns is ultimately responsible for creating successive generations of psychologically damaged children. With an understanding of the contributions of Freud, Erikson, Harlow, Bowlby and Bowen to the field of human development, it makes sense that codependency and the emotional manipulator disorders are linked to a pathological parent-child relationship. It also explains why dysfunctional individual and family patterns are passed down from one generation to the next. Simply stated, children follow their parents' emotional/psychological footsteps.

The eventual manifestation of codependency or an emotional manipulator disorder is directly connected to early childhood psychological damage *perpetrated by a child's emotional manipulator parent.* Emotional manipulators are typically neglectful of their child's basic emotional needs, as their narcissism prevents them from truly understanding and knowing how to unconditionally love and nurture their children. Their narcissism hinders their ability to reliably and regularly make their child feel important, worthwhile and valuable, as their parenting style is selfishly geared towards their own personal and emotional needs. If the child should rebel against or refuse to comply with their parent's self-centered, selfish and rigid parenting expectations, he is at risk of abuse and/or neglect, as narcissists are acutely sensitive and reactive to disappointment.

In the case of the emotional manipulator and codependent parents, the codependent is often unable to protect the child from the harm caused by the emotional manipulator. Although substantially more nurturing and sensitive to their child's emotional needs, the codependent parent's ability to offset the damage perpetrated by the emotional manipulator is limited, as they are typically powerless to protect the child, and for that matter, anyone else in the family. As a direct consequence of the emotional manipulator and codependent parents' psychological limitations and/ or disorders, the child is likely to follow their dysfunctional footsteps. Additional information about the codependent's role in the development of codependency or an emotional manipulator disorder will be presented in the end of the next chapter.

Emotional Manipulators Create Future Codependents

The emotional manipulator parent holds fast to a fantasy that by having a child, his life will be completely transformed. Because of their inherent narcissism, they believe that the manner in which they parent their child, whom they believe will be a perfect cherub baby, will prove to their friends and family that their critical and unfair judgment against them has been wrong. If they create the "perfect" child and are the "perfect" parent, they believe that they will finally prove to the world their real value and worth. Since emotional manipulators are fundamentally shame-based, self-loathing and anxious about being lovable and appreciated, they rely on their child to make them feel competent and worthwhile. The child is consequently burdened by the responsibility of validating and affirming their narcissistic parent. As a consequence, this child is deprived of developing a healthy identity, as they are forced to become an extension of their parent's damaged ego. The child becomes the salve for the emotional manipulator's festering, emotional wounds.

The emotional manipulator parent mistakenly believes that by bringing a new life into the world, he will be able to heal his own childhood wounds and right the wrongs of his own traumatic past. The child is, therefore, unrealistically saddled with the responsibility of undoing or healing his parent's own psychologically damaged childhood. Although the emotional manipulator envisions giving his child the support and protection that he never received, he is rendered incapable by virtue of narcissism. Although this parent believes in the one-dimensional fantasy that love, by itself, will be enough to raise a healthy child, they are thwarted by their own lack of insight and psychological abilities. Their dream of becoming an affirming, nurturing, and loving parent sadly never comes to fruition. Paradoxically, this parent unwittingly transfers their own dark, insecure and unstable past onto their innocent and unprotected child.

Consequently, an unnatural burden is placed on the child of an emotional manipulator to behave in a manner that will make his parent feel better about himself. Because it is impossible for any child to fulfill the emotional manipulator's child-rearing needs and fantasies, the child is naturally subjected to stress and anxiety early in his life. To emotionally cope with his parent's narcissism, the child will attempt to adapt to his parent's interactional style and emotional needs which are neither natural nor developmentally appropriate. If the child is to successfully adapt to his parent's narcissism, he will need to be experienced as a *pleasing* and *accommodating* child. This child's successful adaption will merit him praise and conditional nurturing as he is able to help his parent believe that their parenting fantasies are real.

The Origins of Codependency 71

Codependency is ultimately forged from the child's efforts to independently secure conditional love and attention by pleasing his emotional manipulator parent while also maintaining the fantasy role which was unfairly consigned to him at birth. The child, who can make the parents feel good about themselves and conforms to their fantasies, is likely to be the recipient of praise and conditional love. The child who cannot or will not conform to his emotional manipulators' narcissistic needs will be subjected to much harsher and possibly abusive treatment. The delineation between the development of codependency versus an emotional manipulation disorder is simply the child's ability to make their narcissistic parent feel good about themselves.

Alice Miller, in her book *The Drama of the Gifted Child* (1979), described the unique emotional bind of the child of a narcissistic (emotional manipulator) parent. Dr. Miller used the term "gifted child" to describe children who are able to cope with their narcissistic parent's selfish, self-centered and reactive parenting by developing convoluted, although effective, coping strategies. According to Dr. Miller, the narcissistic parent is an emotionally immature and psychologically damaged individual who uses conditional and manipulative child-rearing practices to fulfill their self-absorbed and selfish needs for attention, validation and acceptance. Children of narcissistic parents survived the harsh realities of their formative years by fulfilling their parent's one-dimensional parent-child fantasy. The "gifted" child, who could coax their narcissistic parent into wanting to care for them, would have been cared for adequately. To encourage their parents to nurture them, it would be required that the child avoid triggering their parent, not be disappointing or become a personal or emotional liability to them. Intuitive children, or as Alice Miller termed "gifted" children, successfully adapt to their narcissistic parents' harmful conditional parenting by developing accurate and reflexive protective responses.

Since the parent, especially the mother, is the child's sole source of survival, the child strives to please, fearing disapproval, or abandonment. Thus, the child sublimates his needs for the parents'. Roles reverse and the child frequently takes on the parent's responsibility as emotional caregiver. This impedes the growth of a child's true identity, and a "loss of self" frequently occurs. The child adapts by not "feeling" his own needs, and develops finely tuned antennae, focusing intensely on the needs of the all-important other.

(Jana L. Perskie, 2003)

Dr. Miller described that as early as infancy, the child of a narcissistic parent intuitively understands and adapts to the parent's narcissistic needs and expectations. The infant learns to relegate his own needs to the back burner, his unconscious mind, in order to maintain a contrived sense of psychological equanimity. Because of the child's learned sensitivity and adaptation to the idiosyncratic and often unpredictable highs and lows of the emotionally unstable narcissistic parent, he is able to create a sense of predictability, safety and ultimately, emotional self-sufficiency. Although this child is essentially denied basic feelings of security and safety – as the narcissistic parent's needs are always more important than his – he still benefits from the conditional forms of love and appreciation that he is given. Emotionally manipulative parents are motivated to care for this child because he makes them feel good about themselves.

The Narcissist's Pleasing Child

Learning to be a "pleasing" or "gifted" child secures the lion's share of their parent's positive attention. Because this child elicits positive attention from others, he will serve to make his parent feel joy and pride. This agreeable, likeable and adorable child will naturally engender praise from others, especially because he is showcased like a trophy. As a complement magnet, the "gifted" child ultimately serves as an extension of his parent's wounded ego and battered self-esteem. Ultimately, this child is subsumed into his parent's ego, as everything he does reflects back to his parent. Instead of being the child who is wonderful and lovable just because he is, instead, he becomes a valued acquisition or trophy of sorts that proves to others their worth and value.

Since the child is considered a natural extension of the emotional manipulator parent, there is little difference between compliments about the parent's looks, a piece of jewelry, her car, or her adorable and talented child. All are treated as objects of the emotional manipulator. Hence, the pleasing child's individuality is absorbed into the emotional manipulator's insatiable need to bring attention back to herself.

The child who is fated to become a codependent will likely be a low maintenance child who reflexively and consistently behaves in a manner that makes the emotional manipulator parent feel whole and competent. The gifted or pleasing child is born into a world that requires him to put his adult parent's needs over his own. After all, making his emotional manipulator parents feel good about themselves is the best way to guarantee that his basic needs are met. Successful adaptation, therefore, requires this child to learn the conditions, although not entirely predictable, that will ensure his parents are content and superficially happy with him.

The child who is destined to become a codependent learns early on that conditional love is much better than no love at all. He also learns the inherent risk in disappointing the emotional manipulator parent, as he has witnessed others who have disappointed and angered his parent and, consequently, became the recipients of his parent's narcissistic rage. The choice between his parent's love and adulation versus their wrath and abuse is clear for this child. He has much invested in perfecting his "pleasing" qualities.

Future codependents develop an instinct for how to behave in order to be perceived as exemplary children. They quickly learn the advantages of staying true to their projected pleasing of gifted persona. They become the child that is always gratifying or pleasing on cue. Maintaining the identity of the fantasy child guise requires them to betray themselves. For example they smile when really wanting to cry, are calm when frightened, comply when they want to rebel, and behave affectionately when angry and resentful.

Pleasing/gifted children must be careful to not be too boastful or showy about any part of their pseudo-self-esteem. If they should accidentally take the spotlight away from their emotional manipulator parent, they might be subject to their parent's resentment, embarrassment, shame or anger – all of which are part of a narcissistic injury. It is, therefore, a challenge for them to walk the very fine line between providing the narcissistic parent with "bragging rights" while not threatening their shallow and unstable personality.

Narcissistic Injuries

The pleasing/gifted child has a great deal riding on his ability to respond quickly and accurately to the emotional manipulator's rapidly fluctuating emotional states. If this child should miscalculate and disappoint, or even worse, embarrass his parent, he is likely to trigger the parent into a narcissistic injury and, consequently, witness or become a victim of his or her fury. A *narcissistic injury* occurs when a narcissist (or an individual with one of the emotional manipulator personality disorders) perceives a situation or direct communication to be threatening and harmful. Narcissists are extremely sensitive to criticism or intolerance of anything perceived as less than perfect performance.

Often the reason for the narcissistic injury is benign and unintended, but the triggering incident is unconsciously and reflexively registered as a threat to the narcissist's fragile self-esteem. From the "injury" comes an intense and aggravated expression of rage, which is commonly known as "narcissistic rage."

"In the aftermath of the NPD person's meltdown, he will often feel an extreme resentment toward you for causing him to lose control. He may even shut you out for a period of time, refusing to speak about the incident again"

(Payson, 2002, p. 24).

Narcissistic rage occurs on a continuum from aloofness, expressions of mild irritation or annoyance to serious outbursts, including violent attacks

(Malmquist, 2006).

To avoid triggering a narcissistic injury and subsequently becoming the target for the emotional manipulator parent's narcissistic rage, the pleasing/gifted child develops a finely-tuned "radar" that quickly and accurately picks up on potentially dangerous emotional situations. This is no ordinary tracking system, as it is so finely tuned that it detects the most subtle shift in an emotional manipulator's emotions or mood – from the barely detectable or disguised to anger or rage. The child's ability to predict, and consequently avoid, his emotional manipulator parent's rapid emotional shifts, is precisely what saves him from being hurt (neglected or abused). Predicting the parents' moods, identifying their triggers, and staying "under the radar" staves off humiliation, deprivation and potential harm. By acutely focusing on the needs of his emotional manipulator parent, and later other narcissists, this child learns that he will be safe from his narcissistic parent's damaging emotional ups and downs. He will learn that his needs will never be as important as those of his emotional manipulator parent and other narcissists in his life.

To manage the "radar system" and emotionally survive his emotionally manipulative parents, the child must learn to split off from his feelings. Without this split, the child would arrive at the emotional realization that he is not worthy of unconditional love and inherently lacking in importance and value. Experiencing the full breadth of his feelings, such as humiliation, fear of aggravated harm, rage or hopelessness, would be too big a blow to his young and fragile mind. Therefore, by pushing these feelings, thoughts and memories into the unconscious mind, or repressing emotionally evocative event(s), the child's mind defends itself from what it is unable to manage and process. Repression is an unconscious protective strategy or defense mechanism that protects the human mind/brain from the deleterious effects of trauma.

Defense Mechanisms

The term defense mechanism was coined by Sigmund Freud in 1894. Defense mechanisms safeguard the mind against feelings, thoughts, memories or even incidents that are perceived as dangerously stressful or anxiety- provoking. Defense mechanisms are the human mind's trauma defense system. They protect a person from fully experiencing trauma by reducing, disguising, redirecting or artificially eliminating it from the conscious experience. These defensive or shielding strategies work because they safeguard a person from the trauma itself or from the experience of humiliation, fear, rage, shame, or even suicidal thoughts.

**All defense mechanisms share two common properties:
they often appear unconsciously and they tend to distort, transform, or
otherwise falsify reality. In distorting reality, there is a change
in perception which allows for a lessening of anxiety, with a corresponding
reduction in felt tension.**

(Straker, 2004)

Defense mechanisms are analogous to circuit breakers. When an electrical system is threatened by a power surge or is overloaded, the circuit breaker is triggered, and consequently diverts or stops the dangerous electrical surge from reaching its destination – the specific electrical device. Without this automatic protective process, electrical devices can be damaged or destroyed, or, even worse, dangerous electrical fires can be ignited. The dangerous surge of electricity would be analogous to a traumatic event or memories of past trauma. Defense mechanisms automatically and reflexively respond to dangerous levels of psychological energy, e.g., a traumatic event that is perceived to endanger a person's emotional survival. For both the electrical and psychological fuse breakers, the circuit will only come back on line when the energy source has been lowered to bearable levels, the energy transferred to a safer place or when the system can tolerate the spike of the increased energy load. In other words, individuals who rely on one or more defense mechanisms to protect them from trauma, past or present, will only consciously experience the trauma when it is safe for them to do so.

Reliance on defense mechanisms is useful to all of us. But there is a price to pay. Although they help buffer and protect a person from trauma, the accumulation of repressed material (memories) often results in a subsequent mental health condition or psychological disorder. Like marbles stuffed in a glass container, a time will come when the container will break. Post-traumatic stress disorder is the most common of these possible disorders. The development of codependency or one of the emotional manipulator disorders is also connected to the chronic need and overuse of defense mechanisms.

Below is a list of Defense Mechanisms (Straker, 2010 and Carter, 2012):

- **Repression:** pushing uncomfortable thoughts into the subconscious.

- **Sublimation:** redirecting 'wrong' urges into socially acceptable actions.

- **Denial:** claiming/believing that what is true is actually false. Unpleasant facts, emotions or events are treated as if they are not real or don't exist.

- **Displacement:** redirecting emotions to a substitute target.

- **Intellectualization:** taking an objective viewpoint.

- **Projection:** attributing uncomfortable feelings to others.

- **Rationalization:** creating false, but credible, justifications.

- **Reaction formation:** converting unconscious wishes or impulses that are perceived to be dangerous into their opposites.

- **Suppression:** painful, frightening or threatening emotions, memories, impulses or drives consciously pushed out of awareness.

- **Conversion:** mental conflict converted to a physical symptom, e.g., a soldier terrified of battle developing paralysis, blindness or deafness with no medical cause.

- **Regression:** giving up current level of development and returning to an earlier level.

- **Fantasy:** retreating into a dream world of times past or changing the focus of a current stressful or anxiety-provoking thought process into unreal or fantasized thoughts.

The child, destined to become a codependent, will go to great lengths to perfect their "pleasing" and "gifted" persona. Out of necessity, they become superb actors in their own life. By becoming believable emotional pretenders, they were able to manage, and to some extent, control their narcissistic parent's emotional fluctuations, while also getting what they needed from them. By successfully feigning or repackaging their real feelings, this child survived her dysfunctional childhood. This "gifted" child endured substantially less emotional trauma than the child who could not or would not successfully fake his way out of harm's way. The "gifted" child, therefore, will likely become an adult who effectively, and at times effortlessly, pretends to be happy when depressed, forgives when resentful or supports when envious. The child will develop into a codependent who will ultimately become a "great pretender."

It is a curious phenomenon when you listen to a song hundreds of times, but never really understood what the lyricist meant to communicate. Such is evident in the following song lyrics, *The Great Pretender*. This song, which was one of my mother's favorites, is actually a very sad song about an adult who learned to act his way out of harm's way. Although ostensibly about a love affair, it could equally be describing a codependent raised by an emotional manipulator.

The Great Pretender
Originally Recorded by the Platters (1955)
By Buck Ram

Oh-oh, yes, I'm the great pretender
Pretending that I'm doing well
My need is such, I pretend too much
I'm lonely, but no one can tell
Oh-oh, yes, I'm the great pretender
Adrift in a world of my own
I've played the game, but to my real shame
You've left me to grieve all alone
Too real is this feeling of make-believe
Too real when I feel what my heart can't conceal
Yes, I'm the great pretender
Just laughin' and gay like a clown
I seem to be what I'm not, you see
I'm wearing my heart like a crown
Pretending that you're still around[11]

Out of necessity, the "pleasing" and "gifted" child becomes an expert at delaying his need for gratification. He makes himself believe that compliments, affirmation, physical affection or other important physical or emotional needs are conditionally tied to making his emotional manipulator artificially feel good about themselves. If this child, a future codependent, cannot embrace this twisted and unnatural rationalization, he may spend his childhood feeling disappointing and worthless. The child who cannot delay his gratification by bending his reality will likely experience anger, resentment, disappointment and shame – all of which will be direct challenges to his psychological survival. Such is the fate of the child who is to become an emotional manipulator.

Surviving the Narcissist Creates Codependency

Children who become codependents move through life with an uncanny ability to comply with unnatural expectations. As master manipulators of their own feelings, they are able to remain calm when frightened, happy when angry and lovable when feeling shameful. Their ability to go against the grain of their own emotions keeps them from further narcissistically injuring their parent, which in turn, may keep them safe from harm. Similar to taking a lemon and making lemonade, a future codependent will be able to "take" a selfish, self-obsessed, critical and abusive parent – an emotional manipulator – and "make" him into a conditionally loving parent. The resourceful and manipulative nature of this child will extend into adulthood. Hence, this child will become the "perfect" match for an intolerant and harmful narcissistic emotional manipulator romantic partner.

The children of emotional manipulators are no different than children who are raised by healthy parents, as all children want to feel good about themselves. The gifted/pleasing child takes great pride in his selfless, sacrificial and unassuming personality. The positive attention, praise and compliments these children receive because of their surrendering, sacrificial and caretaking persona creates pseudo self-esteem and a distorted sense of self-confidence. They are subtly coerced into believing that their sacrifices are noble and for the greater good. To guarantee their narcissistic parent's favor, while avoiding their rejection or wrath, they learn to excel at their adult-like responsibilities. By becoming their sibling's caretaker, the family's cook, the housecleaner, or maintaining a part-time job to help with the family bills, this pleasing child twists her sacrifices into something to be proud of and about which to brag.

This pseudo self-esteem allows her to feel good about a life that is, and always will be, in the shadow of the narcissist. These gifted or pleasing children may never know what they lost as they sacrificed their childhood to make their emotional manipulator parent happy.

As the future codependent child matures, they become the emotional manipulator parent's natural choice to provide care for the family. Because of their dependable, reliable, and, most importantly, compliant nature, these children reluctantly agree to assume the adult responsibilities given to them. They, of course, dare not say no to their parent's requests. They also are "volunteered" for the role of managing their narcissistic parent's emotions. Because children are not hardwired to take on adult challenges and responsibilities, they suffer psychological harm.

Such role reversals are psychologically damaging, as it becomes a forced adult-like relationship for which children are not prepared or capable of. This inappropriate child-adult relationship is referred to as emotional incest. Emotional incest occurs when a parent sabotages a child's intellectual or emotional development by demanding that he partake in deeply personal, intimate and private interactions that are typically reserved for a spouse or adult partner. This includes confiding in children about the adult's personal, occupational, financial or sexual problems, thus putting a damaging burden on the child who is not emotionally equipped to handle it (Kelley and Kelley, 2012).

The gifted/pleasing child endeavors to bolster the emotional manipulator parent's self-esteem by being agreeable, compliant and low-maintenance. These children may also attempt to make their chronically unhappy parent happier by excelling in sports, academics, social activities or work. Overachieving becomes the ego extension that the narcissistic parent requires, as they are void of any real self-esteem. Paradoxically, the child may even strive for premature financial independence in order to ease their parent's burden of caring for them. This future codependent becomes the low maintenance teenager or young adult – the shining star in their parents' life.

As the future codependent matures, their "gifted" and "pleasing" personality is appreciated by more and more people. Other family members, relatives and peers within their social circles not only value their well-developed empathy, listening, and problem-solving abilities, but may also unknowingly take advantage of them. The problem with these "precocious" helpers, listeners and problem solvers is that they never learned the value of caring for themselves. These future codependents naturally and automatically feel comfortable in relationships in which their needs are secondary or ignored, while feeling compelled to take care of someone else. Consequently, they will naturally, if not magnetically, gravitate toward narcissistic or selfish people. Knowing how to care for others, while exhibiting few needs of their own, helped them emotionally survive their challenging life.

It is well known, and an accepted psychological principle, that people are drawn to careers that are a good fit or match with their personality and psychological needs (Roe, 1964). Therefore, it is likely that a future codependent will be attracted to a profession that rewards and values caretaking, patience, empathy, and listening abilities.

> **Perhaps in no other societal system [The United States of America's]**
> **is this positive view of codependent behavior more evident than in**
> **the health care system. The health profession, with its emphasis on devotion**
> **to the care of others, is an ideal medium for the expression**
> **of the nurturing aspects of the codependent person. It has been purported**
> **that many codependent persons become professional caregivers for this**
> **very reason.**
>
> (Clark and Stoffel, 1992, p. 823)

Therefore, it can be expected that children of emotional manipulators, those who survived their childhood because of their "gifted" and "pleasing" qualities/characteristics, will likely be attracted to "helping" careers like psychotherapy, nursing, the clergy and others.

CHAPTER 9
The Origins of Emotional Manipulation Disorders

Children who are raised by healthy and nurturing parents in a safe and secure environment will likely become psychologically healthy adults who experience healthy mutual and reciprocal adult relationships. As explained in the previous chapter, in severely dysfunctional families, children often replicate their parents' psychopathology. Moreover, children carry forward dysfunctional elements of their family of origin into their own relationships or families. As mentioned in the preceding chapter, children of an emotional manipulator parent, who may be partnered with a codependent parent, ultimately repeat the "sins" of their parents, following in their dysfunctional footsteps. In other words, emotional manipulator parents create psychologically damaged children, e.g., codependents (as demonstrated in the last chapter) or emotional manipulators. The deciding factor on which side of the continuum of self the child will find himself is directly influenced by the manner in which he coped and adapted to the emotional manipulator parent. If the child was able to adapt by becoming the gifted or pleasing child, then they will likely become a codependent. And if they could not or were unable to please their parent, they are destined to a harsher and more disturbed future – becoming an emotional manipulator. As they say, "the apple doesn't fall far from the tree." However, in the case of children from emotional manipulator parents, we should ask on which side of the tree does the apple fall?

There are typically two potential outcomes for children raised by emotional manipulators. As illustrated in the preceding chapter, *The Origins of Codependency*, a child who adapted to their emotional manipulator parent by becoming a "pleasing" child will likely become a codependent adult. This "pleasing" and "gifted" child escaped major psychological harm or trauma by behaving in a manner that neither challenged nor disrupted their parent's narcissistic needs or fantasies.

However, for the child who could not or would not fulfill their emotional manipulator parent's narcissistic fantasies, their fate is far bleaker.

Because this child prevented the emotional manipulator parent from actualizing their shallow and ill-conceived narcissistic fantasies of parenthood, they will have been subjected to harsher treatment, e.g., deprivation, neglect, and/or abuse. The child who ruined his parent's veneer thin fantasies, hopes and dreams will most certainly have an uncertain psychological future. This child will likely become an emotional manipulator.

Temperament and Heredity Matter

Because a child's temperament is a product of heredity, a parent can never know what their child's personality will be like. To illustrate, research has revealed that anxiety-related personality traits are 40-60% determined by a child's genes (Emilien et al., 2002). Therefore, there is a significant likelihood that a normal and healthy child could be born with a challenging temperament or personality type. Because of the genetic roulette wheel of personality possibilities, a child who is colicky, stubborn, anxious, attention-challenged or painfully shy will unfortunately be a grave disappointment to their narcissistic parent. Although these children may require more energy and patience, they are still perfectly normal and healthy – at least to psychologically stable parents. However, they might not be treated as such if one of their parents is an emotional manipulator.

Instead of a beautiful and darling bundle of joy that the emotional manipulator parent hoped and dreamed of, they gave birth to a child who was not naturally happy, who could not be soothed and/or who would not or could not fulfill their restrictive one-dimensional narcissistic expectations. The narcissistic parent-child fantasy could have been blown just because the child was the "wrong" gender, had the "wrong" shade or color of skin, didn't look like them, or didn't look and behave like the beautifully perfect babies on their favorite TV commercials. If this child was born with a disfigurement, medical problem or a developmental disability, they would have been even more of a disappointment, if not an outright embarrassment to the emotional manipulator parent.

The emotional manipulator parent reacts to his or her seemingly imperfect child as if a horrible trick was played on them, a bait and switch of sorts. Instead of giving birth to the baby of their dreams, whom they were so sure they would create, they gave birth to a seemingly damaged, ungrateful, difficult and willful child who seemed hell-bent on preventing them from actualizing their long-held fantasies of parenthood. Their hope that a beautiful bundle of joy would deliver them from their own personal misery and traumatic past would most certainly be derailed.

As described in the preceding chapter, the emotional manipulator unconsciously believes their children are an extension of themselves.

In a sense, the narcissist (emotional manipulator) views others and the world around him as an extension of himself, perhaps as you might view your arm or leg...He unconsciously expects you to conform to his will, just as his own arm or leg would do. When your behavior deviates from his expectations, he often becomes as upset with you as he would be if his arm or leg were no longer under his control.

(Payson 2002, p.22)

A "Bad" Child Forever

The emotional manipulator parent will hold a grudge against their seemingly broken and imperfect child who they will forever experience as embarrassing and disappointing. Because of this child's "imperfections," the narcissistic parent's self-serving and selfish needs for affirmation, recognition and praise will not be actualized. This poor and defenseless child will, therefore, be destined to experience a much harsher, more desolate and more neglectful or abusive childhood than the "gifted" and "pleasing" child.

Sadly, the developmental path of the future emotional manipulator adult is more traumatic and psychologically damaging than its gifted counterpart. Since this child is unable to live up to her parental fantasies, she is unfairly labeled as disappointing and difficult – labels that are inaccurate pronouncements of her value to the parent and, ultimately, to herself. This egregiously damaging verdict will eventually become the basis for the child's own self-contempt and deeply damaged self-esteem. Over time, the child will internalize her parent's mistreatment of her and begin to agree with the emotional manipulator parent that she is indeed disappointing, ungrateful and damaged. This is a label that is likely to stick for a lifetime.

Emotional manipulators are reflexively judgmental and reactive to what they perceive as their child's negative traits and deficiencies. It is not that they hate this child; it is more that the child's "imperfections" painfully remind them of what is wrong with themselves – what they hate about themselves that they buried or repressed from their conscious awareness. These parents unknowingly project their own personal shame and disappointment onto their child. As damaged individuals, it is easier to recognize these traits in others, especially their disappointing child, than to see them in themselves.

Emotional manipulators tend to externalize or blame others, especially the child, for their child's acting-out behaviors. They rarely consider the possibility that they actually are the one who is responsible for their child's apparent problems. By blaming others, they are able to escape responsibility for the harm that they perpetrated against their child. Additionally, their failure to take responsibility and to blame others insulates them from knowing and experiencing their parenting deficiencies and failures. Externalizing and blaming away their child's apparent "badness" prevents them from realizing their worst nightmare: They have become the next generation of abusive or neglectful parents who created the next generation of traumatized and damaged children (to become adult emotional manipulators).

When emotional manipulators are unable to tolerate their child's acting- out behaviors, they may resort to punishing or abusing the child. Since this parent takes the acting out personally, and consequently experiences a narcissistic injury, they feel justified in their retaliation. Worse than neglect or deprivation, the narcissistic parent may verbally, emotionally or physically abuse this child. The dreadful reality for this child is that she is being punished for behaving as any child would behave if brought up by a similarly hostile, unsafe and unloving parent. This child will be raised in a perilous environment where she will live in constant fear of triggering her psychologically unpredictable, unstable, and potentially dangerous emotional manipulator parent. Instead of being a natural recipient for unconditional love and kindness, she will be a moving target for unmitigated abuse and neglect.

This child becomes a metaphorical dartboard onto which the emotional manipulator parent hurls darts of disappointment, resentment and even disgust. Since emotional manipulator parents are unable to comprehend their own hatred of themselves, they angrily throw their "darts" of shame, rage and antipathy at the child who unconsciously reminds them of the worst aspects of themselves. One dart at a time, the child absorbs her narcissistic parent's wrath. Over time, she internalizes, or takes on her parent's projected self-loathing, insecurities, lost dreams, broken promises and feelings of abandonment. Sadly, the darts never stop, as the disappointing child is incapable of assuaging her parent's beliefs and assumptions of their inherent inadequacies.

Not only is this "displeasing" and "disappointing" child unable to fulfill the parent's fantasies, her accumulated bitterness manifests in increasingly angry and hostile behaviors, which in turn reinforces the parent's angry, resentful and ultimately distorted view of her. This child is not fighting back per se, but instead just trying to survive a confusing world of mixed messages, broken promises, and horrible disappointment. Because she is in a no-win situation, her acting-out will justify the parent's continued deprivation, neglect and abuse. This unfortunate child is perpetually trapped in a double bind for which there is no way out.

Over time, the displeasing and disappointing child internalizes and identifies with her "bad and disappointing" label. Eventually, this child will likely give up and submit to the inevitable: She will never be able to transform her parent's anger, disappointment and resentment into appreciation, affirmation and most importantly, love. Even if the child could surprise her narcissistic parent and behave as a fantasy child (the pleasing child) should, it would never be enough to change their opinions of her. Paradoxically, if this child should surprise her parent and consistently behave in a "good" and "pleasing" manner, she would be unintentionally challenging her parent's justifications and excuses for their punishing treatment of her. If the emotional manipulator parent's deprivation, neglect, and/or abuse was uncovered and confronted, a defensive, angry and vindictive response would result. The parent would angrily justify their actions, blame others for the child's problems (including the child), and proceed to punish the child further.

Because of prolonged abuse or neglect, this child's negative behaviors will likely escalate in frequency and severity. This cycle of acting-out and punishment results in a perpetual double bind in which the child can never behave in a manner that would stop his emotional manipulative parent's abuse or neglect. Because the child's reactions to the parent's harm are naturally unpleasant, the emotional manipulator feels justified in her actions. Being trapped and not being able to behave in a manner that would stop his parent's abuse, the child has no other option but to behave as the parent expects: angry, resentful, and often vindictive. This unfortunate child will spend his youth in constant fear and dread while unintentionally providing his emotional manipulator parent with distorted justification and rationalization for their harm.

Drew Keys, author of *Narcissists Exposed* (2012), writes on his Lightshouse.org website, about the displeasing and disappointing child who identifies with their mistreatment. Keys refers to this child as a "scapegoat."

Because narcissistic parents cannot accept personal faults, they spend their days trying to convince themselves that everything they do is perfect. When their personality causes distress within their family, and their children's issues begin to reflect this, these parents are forced to make a choice. They must either acknowledge that they are making mistakes that are affecting their children negatively, or they must try to convince themselves and others that the problems are coming not from themselves, but another source...In their minds, by blaming another, they absolve themselves of any wrongdoing, and they can continue to believe – and strive to convince others – that they are in fact, perfect. But they must first have someone to blame...

...For defenseless children made to play scapegoat, the burdens of being labeled "bad" no matter what they do are heavy. The scapegoat soon learns he or she cannot win; there is no sense struggling to improve the family's opinion of them, because that simply cannot be allowed to occur...In a desperate attempt to reduce their parents' active oppression and derision, the scapegoat succumbs to the roles of underachiever, troubled one, loser, black sheep or troublemaker. This presents the parents with exactly what their mental disorder is making them feel they must have – an external object upon which to place blame – so that they can continue the reassuring fantasy that there is nothing wrong with themselves or their family on the whole.

In an effort to alleviate to some degree the distress of her narcissistic mother's wrath, the scapegoat eventually gives in and agrees with the family's assessment of her as inferior and worthy of blame. She internalizes the belief that she is inherently bad, worthless, and defective, and believes that everyone she contacts can clearly see this and will reject her as completely her family does. (Keys, 2012)

Without warmth, acceptance, safety and unconditional love, this child eventually learns that she is essentially unlovable, unworthy and that the world is an unsafe place. Humiliation, shame and anger accumulate as she realizes that the abuse and neglect may never stop and unconditional love will never come. To temper the child's loss of hope and despair, and to survive her living nightmare, she will need a psychological strategy to protect her from the stark realities of her life. Such protection can be attained through the use of a wide array of defense mechanisms.[12] This child defends herself by the same defense mechanisms as would a person who was violently traumatized, e.g., by rape, war trauma or witnessing a murder.

---

[12] Defenses listed in the previous chapter.

Repression and Disassociation: The Brain's Circuit Breaker

The human mind has distinct limits to how much trauma it can manage. Analogous to the previously mentioned circuit breaker analogy, the human mind has properties that protect it from experiences that are too painful and threatening to manage. It's virtual on and off switch or circuit breaker protects a person from what he is unable to process and subsequently store in short-term memory. Repression and disassociation are the primary defense mechanisms that help a person manage unbearable trauma. Repression is defined as the unconscious exclusion of painful impulses, desires, or fears from the conscious mind. When a traumatic episode is repressed, a person simply forgets that it ever happened. Disassociation is defined as the psychological experience in which people feel disconnected from their sensory experience, sense of self or personal history. One of several forms of disassociation is to feel that one is looking down at oneself while the abuse is happening.

Repression and disassociation are essential to the psychological survival of most trauma victims, especially the neglected and abused child of an emotional manipulator parent. Without these defenses, the child, and the adult he will become, will not only remember the trauma, but will also emotionally re-experience the debilitating shame, anger, loss of hope and desperation that they experienced during the trauma. Because the resulting embarrassment, shame, self-hatred, neediness and the expansive reservoirs of rage are too unbearable to accept (consciously experience), they are consigned to the dark expanses of the unconscious mind, locked behind iron-reinforced concrete walls of denial –resisting any attempts at expression or recovery. These repressed feelings (and memories) will only see the light of day through bouts of deep depression, narcissistic rage or with experienced psychotherapists.

As a consequence of their traumatic history and the resulting psychological damage, these psychologically impaired children will grow up and become adults who are unable to create or sustain healthy romantic relationships. More specifically, their abusive and neglectful childhoods will manifest in a mental health disorder, notably one of the three emotional manipulator personality disorders. As an emotional manipulator, they will naturally be hyper-focused on getting their needs met first or being adept at getting others to meet their needs without feeling compelled to reciprocate. As narcissists, they will be oblivious to any harm they cause other people.

The childhoods of these emotional manipulators proved that only through a selfish and egotistic approach to others (relationships) could they feel good about themselves. The ability to manipulate or exploit others, combined with an exaggerated sense of their own importance, helped them to survive their traumatic childhood. Forming healthy, reciprocal, and mutually reinforcing attachments is not likely ever to occur, as this future emotional manipulator's will unknowingly follows the dysfunctional and harming path of the parents that created them. In a manner of speaking, they are "cursed" to follow in the very same psychopathological footsteps as the parent that abused and neglected them.

The Subjective Nature of Trauma

To explain why some individuals with narcissistic personality disorder come from families (parents) who did not treat them harshly or abusively, it is necessary to explain the subjective nature of trauma. I have often explained to my clients, and those who I have clinically supervised, that trauma is not defined by what happens to a person, but instead, by their personal experience of it. For example, if a child who was lost in the mix of an emotional manipulator parent's personal or psychological absence, such as depression, lack of motivation to bond or physical absence, they are more likely to suffer the fate of the abused child. This deprived or neglected child similarly experiences a dark, unloving and emotionally-barren childhood in which she internalizes feelings and beliefs of inadequacy, unimportance and unworthiness.

Similarly, an emotional manipulation disorder (and codependency) can be caused by a sterile, neglectful or unsafe childhood environment that resulted from absent parents, a debilitating medical or mental illness, poverty or living in an unsafe crime-infested community. Living in a neglectful or abusive orphanage, foster home, military school, boarding school or other similar emotionally scarring environments may also result in adult psychopathology, such as an emotional manipulation disorder.

Although I have presented a viable and sensible explanation for the origins of both codependency and the emotional manipulation disorders, it is important to inform the reader that, in this author's opinion, it is not possible to account for every and all circumstances, conditions, or factors that are responsible for these disorders. Moreover, it is not written in stone that emotional manipulators always create codependent or emotional manipulator children. There may be mitigating circumstances that offset the child's early traumatic experiences with their emotionally manipulative parent. For example, if the emotional manipulator parent relied on childcare from an adult caregiver who was consistently loving and nurturing to the child, then the child's traumatic early-life experiences may have been sufficiently offset. Such a substitute parent could include a relative caregiver, a nanny or a long-term babysitter. Even an involved and caring coach or teacher could have sufficiently buffered the damage caused by an emotional manipulator parent. An older sibling who took on the role of a protective, nurturing and affirming parent substitute might have similarly offset the possibility for the development of adult psychopathology, such as codependency or an emotional manipulator disorder.

The Codependent Parent's Role

Per this book's thesis, if one parent is an emotional manipulator and they have a long-term romantic partner, i.e., a spouse, then it is assumed the other parent is a codependent. Often in my seminars, I am asked about the codependent parent's role in their child's development of either codependency or an emotional manipulation disorder. The question arises: Can a loving and caring codependent parent offset the deprivation, neglect or abuse perpetrated against their child by their emotional manipulator spouse? Although codependent parents are capable of nurturing their children, their ability to buffer the harm caused by their emotionally manipulative partners is offset by their inability to control their partner's harmful treatment of the family – especially the children. By definition and through this author's own clinical experience, codependent parents are typically unable to control or protect their child from the majority of the harm caused by the emotional manipulator parent.

In actuality, the codependent shares responsibility for the child's harm. Although it could be argued that the codependent is also a victim of the emotional manipulator, it is unfair to any child to excuse away a parent's inability to protect them because they just couldn't or because they similarly considered themselves a victim. Often in the beginning of therapy, my codependent clients cannot wrap their arms around the concept that their "wonderfully loving and nurturing" codependent parent should share any blame in their neglectful or abusive childhood. When they are ready and able to understand that their codependent parent shared some level of responsibility for the harm perpetrated against them, and they are subsequently able to reconcile the idealization and the reality of their codependent parent, then they are able to move even further along their healing therapy journey.

Lastly, a codependent parent who does not subject her child to an emotional manipulator parent, e.g., a single parent who doesn't remarry, may or may not harm her child to the point of becoming a codependent adult. The reason for this is beyond the scope of this book.

CHAPTER 10

Codependency

Even though the book is written about *both* codependency and the emotional manipulation disorders, as well as the attraction dynamics shared by the two, it is clearly more oriented towards codependency. As mentioned in several chapters, this book is deeply and unavoidably influenced by both my personal struggles with codependency, as well as my work with my codependent clientele. When I take a few steps back and reflect upon my life, I am humbled by the extraordinary forces that chiseled out my present psychological and emotional form. It is clear that my efforts to overcome the vice-like grip that codependency had on my life ultimately defined me as a person and as a professional. I am sincerely grateful for my struggles with codependency, as it ultimately paved the way for me to be a healthier and happier person, while being a more sympathetic, empathetic and effective psychotherapist.

It is expected that the codependent reader, more than the emotional manipulator reader, will experience this book as an inviting and useful resource for their personal growth. Because codependents are capable of seeking outside help for their personal, relational and emotional problems, they are consequently more likely to read a book like this. Codependents, and those who are seeking help for imbalanced or dysfunctional personal relationships, will more than likely respond to this book with an open mind, while appreciating its relevance. Conversely, it has been my experience that emotional manipulators respond to my seminar and articles I have written about codependency and the emotional manipulation disorders with defensiveness, contempt and anger. I surmise that these topics cause an unintended narcissistic injury.

This book is likely to resonate strongly with those in the helping professions, as many have struggled with codependency and have been in relationships with emotional manipulators. To illustrate, a 1985-1986 poll conducted by the Arizona-based Sierra Tucson Treatment Center, revealed that 25% of the persons seeking treatment for codependency worked in the field of human services (Laign, 1989). Codependency is more prevalent in the helping professions, specifically the health care and the psychotherapy fields. This is not coincidental. Perhaps in no other societal system is this positive view of codependent behavior more evident than in the health care system. The health care and mental health professions, with their emphasis on devotion to the care of others, are an ideal medium for the expression of the nurturing aspects of the codependent person. It has been purported that many codependent persons become professional caregivers for this very reason (Clark & Stoffel, 1991).

Conversely, it is unlikely that emotional manipulators will appreciate this or similar books due to their tendency to be defensive and reactive to insinuations or direct comments about their mental health. Since their fragile self-esteem cannot tolerate the idea that they share responsibility for their dysfunctional relationship, they are likely to experience this book as blaming, unsympathetic and simply wrong. Although emotional manipulators have suffered more than their codependent counterparts, it is exponentially more difficult for them to explore the root of their problems. To do so would unearth a long-hidden reservoir of intensely painful repressed memories.

I have observed an interesting pattern during my "Codependents and Emotional Manipulators: Understanding the Attraction" seminar circuit. Typically, one or two participants become angry and agitated by the presentation. According to their verbal and/or written feedback, they feel the seminar is offensive, ill-conceived, biased and even absurd. In particular, they are quite bothered by what they perceive as prejudice. These participants hear me say that codependents are the victims and emotional manipulators are the perpetrators of their dysfunctional relationships. Nothing could be further from the truth, as the training (and this book) specifically details how both the codependent and the emotional manipulator are equally willing magnets in their dysfunctional "dance." The codependent's tendency to find harmful partners and remain with them cannot and should not be blamed on emotional manipulators, or vice versa.

It would appear that the severe reactions from my audience are likely products of a narcissistic injury, which occurs when the narcissistic individual *felt* criticized, judged or defeated. If this is accurate, these participants are probably unconsciously triggered by the content of the seminar because they are moderately to severely self-oriented or narcissistic individuals, having a CSV of (+4) or (+5). Anger and defensiveness are the common reactions of a narcissistically-injured emotional manipulator, as they *feel* offended, degraded and/or humiliated when confronted about their wrongdoings. Incidentally, I do not think that negative feedback to either this book or my seminars automatically translates to a person's being an emotional manipulator.

Codependency: An Overused, Misused and Misunderstood Term

Regrettably, the term "codependency" has been overused, misused and often misunderstood. It has become a caricature of its original meaning. To the general public, the term now implies that a person is weak, needy, clingy and even emotionally sick. Like the term "dysfunctional," it has been lazily and conveniently reshaped to fit our mainstream lexicon. Unfortunately, when the media and general public use diagnostic terminology outside the contexts for which it was created, the intended meaning is often lost or diluted.

The roots of the condition that would eventually be referred to as "codependency" are in the Alcoholics Anonymous (AA) movement, which was established in 1936. Since physicians were the early pioneers of alcohol treatment, alcoholism was naturally conceptualized according to the medical model, which approached all addictions in the same manner as a physician would approach a disease or physical ailment, which is to focus primarily on the individual's ailment and how it affects their internal systems. By embracing the medical model, or as many in the 12-Step field refer to it, the disease model, the enduring nature of alcoholism made greater sense. It was no longer seen as a personality weakness or character deficiency, but as a bona fide medical problem.

Although it took a few decades, the addiction treatment field would eventually catch up with AA which, as early as 1951, started Al-Anon, a 12-Step recovery program for the families and significant others of the alcoholic. Al-Anon addressed the other side of the alcoholism coin – the suffering family members who, like the alcoholic, felt like their lives were out of control and littered with obstacles and losses.

"The development of Al-Anon followed that of Alcoholics Anonymous, as naturally as spring follows winter, because where the alcoholics met, the wives met too, made the tea and shared their terrible secret of living with alcoholism. It was while they talked to each other that they realized that they too had been affected and also needed a program of recovery."

(www.alanon.org.za, 2012)

By the 1970s, alcohol treatment providers began to consider the limitations of the medical model, especially when it was used as the only treatment modality. They began to understand the necessity of including the social, familial and relational aspects of the alcoholic's life. Therefore, until the early 1970s, the alcoholic's partners and family were not regularly included in the treatment process. By including the family and significant others of the alcoholic/addict in the treatment process, better outcomes (lower recidivism rates) were achieved.

As a result of the groundbreaking drug and alcohol treatment initiatives of the 1970s, which were heavily influenced by AA and Al-Anon, alcohol treatment programs began to focus on the family and significant other dynamics that contributed to the addiction. Eventually, the family and significant others of the addict/alcoholic were both considered and included in the treatment process. In the 1980's, addiction treatment programs began to regularly provide services to the families and partners of the alcoholic or addict. By the 1990's, most drug treatment programs either required or highly recommended some level of family and significant other participation. As addiction treatment centers took into account the family's role in both the disease and its treatment, outcomes naturally improved.

With the involvement of family members and the partners of the alcoholic, the treatment terminology broadened. Terms like "adult-child of an alcoholic," "alcoholic families" and "co-alcoholic" were created to keep up with the advances in drug and alcohol treatment. "Co-alcoholic" was the preferred, and perhaps more accurate, term to describe the partner of the alcoholic (literally means the partner to the alcoholic). Since drug addictions and alcoholism shared more similarities than differences, beginning in the early to mid-1980s, the various drug treatment programs began to merge into one unified program. "Chemical dependency" became the term of choice as it better reflected the fact that alcohol was indeed a drug (chemical) and, therefore, should not be treated differently from other drug addictions. Consequently, treatment for all addictions coalesced into a unified treatment paradigm, "chemical dependency." Eventually, the term co-alcoholic was updated to codependent – the partner of the chemically-*dependent* individual. Similarly, "co-alcoholism" was replaced by "codependency."

The change in terminology caused some confusion as many incorrectly interpreted the new term as having more to do with a dependent personality type who joined another dependent person in a relationship – two dependents or co-dependents. Instead, "codependency" denoted a person who was habitually in relationships with chemically dependent individuals, whom they would try to control, but were ultimately powerless to. Because of the confusion about the term itself, which continues to the present day, there have been numerous incorrect assumptions and connotations about the term/disorder.

By the early 1980s, codependency was used only to describe a person who was habitually in relationships with chemically dependent partners. A person was considered to be a codependent if they were (a) in a love or marital relationship with an alcoholic, (b) had one or more alcoholic parents or grandparents, or (c) were raised within an emotionally repressive family (Wegscheider-Cruse, 1984). Chemical dependency treatment facilities started to regularly provide treatment and/or support services to the alcoholic's (addict's) family members. Their primary focus with the codependents and/or significant others of the addict, was to support them during the treatment process while teaching them about their role in the problem, or the disease. Over time the term "codependency" became increasingly more accepted within the treatment and psychotherapeutic fields. It would eventually become the standard diagnostic term used for the chemically dependent individual's partner or other individuals who enabled a chemically dependent friend/loved one.

By the mid 1980s, thanks to many key advances within the chemical dependency fields, including the proliferation of research and books on the topic, the term "codependency" was further broadened, reshaped and refined. The meaning of the term was expanded to describe an individual who was habitually in relationships with narcissistic or addicted individuals. The layman and professionals alike began to use the term "codependency" to describe a person who could not or would not adequately care for or fulfill their own emotional and personal needs, while hyper-focusing on the needs, desires and requests of others. According to the revised definition, codependents habitually demonstrated people-pleasing or sacrificial interpersonal behaviors while feeling powerless to resist relationships with addicted, controlling and/or narcissistic individuals. It became evident that codependents came from all walks of life and were not necessarily only married or in a relationship with chemically-dependent/addicted individuals.

A 1986 groundbreaking book by Melody Beattie, *Codependent No More: How to Stop Controlling Others and Start Caring for Yourself,* was instrumental in promoting a greater understanding of what is now seen as a universal problem. Her pioneering codependency book sold over 8 million copies worldwide.

The sales of the book suggest that codependency is a problem that spans regional, ethnic, and cultural boundaries. As a result of Ms. Beattie's book, as well as a host of other important literary and research related contributions on the subject, codependency, the disorder, finally saw the light of day. It came out of the closet and was no longer considered a shameful secret for which there was no help. Books like *Codependent No More* helped change the world's attitudes for the partners of addicts or narcissists. Codependents were no longer viewed as weak and defenseless victims who were powerless to leave their harmful and dysfunctional relationships. By the end of the 1980s, codependency treatment options became increasingly available to help these individuals to free themselves from habitual and harmful relationships.

Codependents Anonymous

At about the same time *Codependent No More* was published, Co-Dependents Anonymous (CODA) was established. CODA is an Alcoholics Anonymous-like organization that promotes a 12-Step recovery process by which individuals can find an ongoing solution to their out-of-control and destructive codependency tendencies. As an organization, CODA strives to help codependents develop healthy and self-empowering relationships. It is estimated that CODA is active in more than 40 countries, with approximately 1,200 active groups in the United States alone.

Because codependency shares many similarities with alcoholism and the other addictions, CODA effectively utilizes the Alcoholics Anonymous 12-Step program. Alcoholics and other addicts are unable to stop their addictive behavior, which they compulsively seek because of its pleasurable properties, but cannot control. As a result of their uncontrollable drug addiction, the addict's life becomes strewn with negative consequences and subsequently spirals out of control. Similarly, codependents seek to control others, who, by their very nature, cannot be controlled. Like an alcoholic's relationship to alcohol, codependents similarly believe they can control their narcissistic or chemically-dependent partner, who they believe has the capacity to make them feel happy. Codependents habitually and compulsively find themselves on a hamster wheel of relationship possibilities – always trying to control the uncontrollable, but never really getting anywhere.

The similarities of AA and CODA are exemplified by their first steps (of the 12-Steps):

"We admitted we were powerless over alcohol – that our lives had become unmanageable." versus "We admitted we were powerless over others – that our lives had become unmanageable."

(Alcoholics Anonymous World Service, 1939)

Both addictions and codependency are progressive processes that are characterized by losses, negative consequences, denial and an urge to control something or someone, that can never be controlled. CODA's 12-Step recovery model as well as the other "Anonymous" 12-Step groups are quite beneficial to individuals, codependents, who feel desperately out of control with their compulsion to control their addicted or emotionally manipulative partner. This is why I often recommend CODA to my codependent clients. It should be noted that CODA does not replace therapy nor does therapy replace 12-Step work.

Since the understanding and treatment of codependency has evolved over the last 30 years, it may be helpful to understand the problem from other perspectives. The following are a handful of definitions that are consistent with my own experiences with codependency.

To start, the Merriam Webster Online Dictionary defines codependency as:

…a psychological condition or a relationship in which a person is controlled by another who is affected with a pathological condition (as in an addiction to alcohol or heroin); and in broader terms, it refers to the dependence on the needs of or control of another.

In Clark & Stoffel's 1992 research article entitled, "Assessment of Codependency Behavior in Two Health Student Groups," they described/defined codependency as:

"A pattern of painful dependence on compulsive behaviors and others' approval in an attempt to find safety, self-worth, and identity."

"…a progressive process whereby self-denial and concomitant caring for other family members is based on the assumption that doing so will foster love, closeness, acceptance, and security in the family."

"…an extreme sense of responsibility to others, inability to appropriately care for the self, increased focus on others' needs, decreased focus on needs of the self, overreaction to things external to the self, under-reaction to things internal to the self, low self-esteem, low self-concept, high external locus of control, and denial"

(p. 822).

"(A willingness) to sacrifice so much of themselves that they set aside their own physical, emotional, and psychological needs for the sake of others. They are detrimentally selfless"

(p. 823).

According to Melody Beattie's landmark book *Codependent No More* (1986):

> **"A codependent person is one who has let another person's behavior affect him or her, and who is obsessed with controlling that person's behavior"**
>
> (p.34).

> **"Codependency involves a habitual system of thinking, feeling, and behaving toward ourselves and others that can cause us pain. Codependent behaviors or habits are self-destructive"**
>
> (p. 37).

> **"We (codependents) frequently react to people who are destroying themselves; we react by learning to destroy ourselves. These habits can lead us into, or keep us in, destructive relationships, relationships that don't work. These behaviors can sabotage relationships that may otherwise have worked. These behaviors can prevent us from finding peace and happiness with the most important person in our lives – ourselves. These behaviors belong to the only person each of us can control – the only person we can change – ourselves"**
>
> (p. 37).

> **"Codependency is many things. It is a dependency on people – on their moods, behaviors, sickness or well-being, and their love. It is a paradoxical dependency. Codependents appear to be depended upon, but they are dependent. They look strong but feel helpless. They appear controlling, but in reality are controlled themselves, sometimes by an illness such as alcoholism"**
>
> (pp. 51-52).

According to this author, codependency is a problematic relationship orientation which involves the relinquishing of power and control to individuals who are either addicted or who have one of the three emotional manipulation personality disorders. In other words, codependents habitually find themselves in relationships with egotistic, self-centered, selfish, and/or addicted individuals. Codependents are habitually and magnetically attracted to people who neither seem interested nor motivated to participate in mutual or reciprocal relationships. Additionally, codependents willingly participate in relationships in which there is an unfair distribution of love, respect, and care, both given and received. By habitually choosing narcissistic or addicted friends or romantic partners, codependents consistently feel unfulfilled, disrespected and undervalued. As much as they resent and complain about the inequity in their relationships, codependents feel powerless to change them.

Codependency Subtypes: Passive Versus Active

There are two subtypes of codependency: passive and active. Although all codependents are habitually and instinctively attracted (and later bonded) to severely narcissistic partners, one is more active in their perpetual but unsuccessful attempts to obtain their emotional manipulator's love, respect and care (LRC), while the other is more passive. Although both try to control and manipulate their narcissistic partners into meeting their LRC needs, they go about it differently.

Passive codependents are more fearful and avoidant of conflict. For complicated reasons, mostly related to their extremely low self-esteem, fear of being alone and tendency to be in relationships with controlling, dangerous and/or abusive emotional manipulators, the passive codependent attempts to control or influence their narcissistic partner through carefully, if not meticulously, executed control strategies – most of which are intended to fall under their emotional manipulator's radar (awareness). Because of the secret and hidden nature of their control strategies, passive codependents are perceived as more manipulative (than active codependents).

Active codependents, on the other hand, more boldly and overtly attempt to manipulate their narcissistic partner into meeting their LRC needs. Being less afraid of conflict and subsequent harm, they are prone to initiate arguments and confrontations with emotional manipulators. Active codependents are often mistaken for narcissists because of their more openly controlling demeanor. Even though they are caught in a never winning cycle of trying to control someone who is neither interested nor capable of meeting their LRC needs, they are typically not able or motivated to end the relationship. Like the passive codependent, they believe that "one day" their pathologically narcissistic partner will realize their mistakes and wrong-doings and finally give them the love, respect and care they so desperately want and need. It just never happens...

Although different "on the outside," both the passive and active codependent share the pathological "others" self-orientation. They both remain with pathologically narcissistic partners while being unhappy, angry and resentful at the lack of reciprocity, mutuality and fairness in their relationship. While the active codependent may seem stronger, more in control and more confident, both share the same deeply imbedded insecurities and feelings of powerlessness. Both are unable to break free from their dysfunctional relationship.

Many readers and seminar participants have asked why I only consider emotional manipulators to be emotionally manipulative, not codependents. That couldn't be further from the truth. This is where it is important to remind the reader that the diagnostic term used in this book, "emotional manipulator," is specifically defined as an individual who fits the diagnostic criteria for one of three personality disorders: Borderline, Narcissistic, or Antisocial and/or is addicted to a drug or process (e.g., sex or gambling). Emotional manipulators, as defined in the book, are pathologically narcissistic.

The phrase "emotionally manipulative" or "emotional manipulator" is just one of countless personality descriptions that could fit almost anyone, including codependents. All of us, healthy or not, have the capacity to be emotionally manipulative. Hence, codependents can also be emotionally manipulative or described as emotional manipulators. However, the diagnostic term "emotional manipulator" is only used for the aforementioned pathological narcissists and/or addicts.

According to the continuum of self theory, codependency is represented on the continuum as a (-5) continuum of self value or CSV. Their "others" self-orientation is expressed as a complete willingness to give love, respect and caring (LRC) to their relationship partners, without the hope or the possibility of receiving the same in return. Codependents feel chemistry or intense attraction to individuals with an opposite self-orientation (inversely matching CSVs). They typically choose emotional manipulators as relationship partners, whose emotional and personal needs and desires supersede their own.

The Human Magnet Syndrome

According to the human magnet explanation, codependents are "magnetically" attracted to emotional manipulators because of their opposite "magnetic polarity." As the north pole of a magnet is always attracted to the south pole of another magnet, so will codependents always be attracted to emotional manipulators. Magnetic roles, like compatible CSVs, are inversely and proportionally attracted to each other. Therefore, codependents are attracted to individuals who are either narcissistic or addicted and who neither want nor are able to fulfill their personal and emotional needs. Conversely, human magnets are always repelled by their own personality type.

From this author's vantage point, codependency is both a personality type and a pattern of dysfunctional behavior. Codependents are habitually attracted to emotional manipulators and/or those who have an addiction. Consequently, they are typically involved in unhealthy or dysfunctional relationships in which they are both quantitatively and qualitatively more generous, patient and forgiving than their partners. Their "give and take ratio" is always lopsided toward the "give." Codependents believe if they are just patient, loving and forgiving enough, eventually their emotionally manipulative or addicted partner will come to their senses, and realize and regret their selfishness and harmful ways. The problem with this belief system is that it is based on flawed logic and distorted thinking. Just as "you can't squeeze blood from a turnip," it is impossible for the codependent to force the emotional manipulator to be that which they are not: unconditionally generous, supportive and empathic.

Codependents cannot shake the unrealistic belief that happiness will only come if they are in a relationship. They look to other people to make them feel happy and fulfilled. It is only through an intimate relationship that they will be able to feel complete. Codependents tend to rely on a source outside of themselves – their romantic partners – to make them feel worthwhile and lovable. This type of expectation doesn't ever materialize because codependents are naturally attracted to the other side of the disordered coin – an emotional manipulator. It is as if they, a "half person," are seeking another "half person" in hopes of creating a "whole relationship." Alas, the relationship math doesn't work. It takes two healthy or whole individuals, to make a fundamentally healthy and lasting relationship. In this case only, one half and one half doesn't equal one whole. My apologies to the field of mathematics!

As a result of the codependent's reliance on emotional manipulators to make them feel good about themselves, they seldom experience self-love or healthy levels of self-esteem. They hold fast to the conviction that their partner, who is inherently incapable of mutuality, empathy or unconditional love, will eventually turn a corner and become the type of person who will be motivated to unconditionally love, respect and care for them. Sadly, they end up waiting a very long time before learning that their hopes and desires never come to fruition. Codependents simply believe in the impossible. Even with mounting consequences, losses and feelings of desperation and isolation, codependents continue their pursuit of what they believe they deserve but can never seem to obtain. They are controlled by the analogous idea that the "carrot" they so ardently crave always seems within their grasp, but in all actuality is unattainable. They may spend a lifetime unsuccessfully chasing their narcissistic "carrot."

Emotional manipulators are simply not interested, willing or capable of fulfilling their codependent partner's needs unless they somehow derive some level of benefit.

Since the codependent unconsciously chooses partners who are unwilling, unmotivated or unable to meet their personal and emotional needs, they may choose the path of control to get their emotional manipulator partner to give them what they want and need. To some, it is counterintuitive for codependents to be controlling. There are indeed codependents who do give up and take a passive victim-based role in their dysfunctional relationships. However, because most codependents take on the lion's share of the relationship responsibilities such as child care, house cleaning, cooking, shopping, and/or financially supporting the relationship/family, they cannot afford to acquiesce and relinquish control of their family's life. Without maintaining some semblance of control, they and their family or relationship would certainly suffer. To most codependents, the idea of stopping their attempts to get their narcissist partner to reciprocate or behave fairly and responsibly is tantamount to giving up on their relationship; something that codependents are mostly unwilling and incapable of doing.

An Addictive-Like Pattern

Codependents often develop compulsive or addictive-like patterns while trying to control their emotionally manipulative partner. Their compulsion to control someone who cannot be controlled puts them on a circular path that always brings them back to where they started: angry, frustrated and resentful. Much like the hamster on its wheel, they run around and around trying to get somewhere, but always end up in the same place. No matter how fast and how long they run, they never actually leave the place where they started – their dysfunctional relationship with an emotional manipulator. Their attempts to seek the unobtainable create a series of personal and relational failures that ultimately remind them of their powerlessness over others. This pattern is self-reinforcing. The more they fail at controlling the emotional manipulator, the worse they feel. Over time, they get worn down by their failures and consequently give up on the hope that they will ever be nurtured, appreciated and affirmed.

Codependents are slow to give up hope that their partner will eventually give them what they want, deserve and need. However, for some codependents, their patience eventually runs thin. Their naïve belief that their emotionally manipulative partner will give them what they have so sacrificially and patiently been waiting for eventually transforms into bouts of anger and resentment. Realizing that hoping and waiting does not get them what they want, i.e., their spouse to be stop drinking, stop an affair, or to show them love and thoughtfulness, they resort either to direct or passive forms of aggression. Instead of running on their hamster wheel, they start to actively attempt to control their unyielding partner. So the stereotype that codependents are passive victims who wait a lifetime to get what they want is just not true.

Co-dependents Anonymous breaks down the characteristics of codependency into five patterns: denial patterns, low self-esteem patterns, compliance patterns, control patterns and avoidance patterns.

The Patterns and Characteristics of Codependents

Denial Patterns

- I minimize, alter or deny how I truly feel.

- I perceive myself as completely unselfish and dedicated to the well-being of others.

Low Self-Esteem Patterns

- I have difficulty making decisions.

- I judge everything I think, say or do harshly, as never "good enough."

- I am embarrassed to receive recognition, praise or gifts.

- I do not ask others to meet my needs or desires.

- I value others' approval of my thinking, feelings and behavior over my own.

- I do not perceive myself as a lovable or worthwhile person.

Compliance Patterns

- I compromise my own values and integrity to avoid rejection or others' anger.

- I am very sensitive to how others are feeling and feel the same.

- I am extremely loyal, remaining in harmful situations too long.

- I value others' opinions and feelings more than my own and am afraid to express differing opinions and feelings of my own.

- I put aside my own interests and hobbies in order to do what others want.

- I accept sex when I want love.

Control Patterns

- I believe most other people are incapable of taking care of themselves.

- I attempt to convince others of what they "should" think and how they "truly" feel.

- I become resentful when others will not let me help them.

- I freely offer others advice and directions without being asked.

- I lavish gifts and favors on those I care about.

- I use sex to gain approval and acceptance.

- I have to be "needed" in order to have a relationship with others.

Avoidance Patterns

- I act in ways that invite others to reject, shame, or express anger toward me.

- I judge harshly what others think, say, or do.

- I avoid emotional, physical, or sexual intimacy as a means of maintaining distance.

- I allow my addictions to people, places, and things to distract me from achieving intimacy in relationships.

- I use indirect and evasive communication to avoid conflict or confrontation.

- I diminish my capacity to have healthy relationships by declining to use all the tools of recovery.

- I suppress my feelings or needs to avoid feeling vulnerable.

- I pull people toward me, but when they get close, I push them away.

- I refuse to give up my self-will to avoid surrendering to a power that is greater than myself.

- I believe displays of emotion are a sign of weakness.

- I withhold expressions of appreciation.

Typical Codependency Traits:

- Low self-esteem

- Self-worth/self-esteem is dependent on being needed and having few needs

- Excessively compliant to suggestions, requests or inappropriate orders

- Preoccupied with the problems, struggles and needs of others, while neglecting their own

- In an attempt to be everything to everybody, loses ability to take care of their own needs

- A champion and avid supporter of the needs, goals and dreams of others while ignoring or devaluing their own

- Adept at solving the problems of others while not being able or motivated to solve their own

- Perpetual people pleasers, always looking to help or "lend a hand"

- Struggles at declining a request for help – may feel guilty or needy

- Over-commitment in many important relationships

- Cannot say no to requests for help

- Creates excessive/impossible work and personal schedule

- Unable to ask for what they want or need

- Feels "selfish" or "needy" when asking for help

- Feels bad or guilty when saying no to a request for help

- Difficulty identifying and communicating emotions

- Willingly conforms to unrealistic and unreasonable relationship expectations

- Fearful and avoidant of disagreements and conflict

- Feels powerless to protect themselves from harm; easily manipulated and exploited by self-serving individuals

- Does not set firm boundaries (consequences) when mistreated and/ or abused

- Attempts to control or manipulate others who typically neglect them

- In an attempt to be helpful, pushes their "help" onto others

- Confuses work and personal relationships

Some codependents rationalize or repackage their codependency traits into positive behaviors. Their codependency becomes a badge of honor of sorts, to be worn proudly – and often. These individuals experience what I refer to as the "codependent martyr syndrome." The codependent martyr is intensely proud of their selfless, sacrificial, and long-suffering approach to their relationships. Their identity and self-esteem becomes fused with their codependency. These martyrs are proud and even boastful about how much they do for others as well as how much they sacrifice in their lives. These belief patterns are often impacted by their family values that are passed down from one generation to the next. This transgenerational pattern is often influenced by regional, ethnic, cultural or religious beliefs and practices.

The martyr's self-esteem, or what I refer to as pseudo self-esteem, is built on a foundation of compliments. In other words, their codependency is reinforced by the positive attention, recognition and even awards they receive for their selflessness. As individuals who ask for very little and are always there to help others, they may be referred to as a "real saint" or the "salt of the earth." If asked why they do not ask for much, they are likely to say they really do not need much and giving to others makes they feel happy and fulfilled. Many even rationalize their selfless, giving, and generous nature as necessary to the path for religious salvation or a guarantee of an eternal afterlife. They not only sacrifice like no other, they won't let you forget about it either. Some codependent martyrs generously provide guilt trips to remind others of their sacrifice.

CHAPTER 11

Narcissistic Personality Disorder (NPD)

It seems that individuals with moderate levels of narcissism are praised or rewarded in our society. Traits such as brash and bold self-confidence, over the top self-promotion, and a desire to be noticed and appreciated are valued American traits. In the book, *The Culture of Narcissism: American Life in an Age of Diminishing Expectations* (1991), Christopher Lasch explained that following World War II, the American culture turned its focus inward towards the only thing it could hope to control – itself. As a result of post-World War II economic wealth, liberal government/politics, the disintegration of organized religion and a society seeking self-actualization, the American people divested themselves of their community-based social values and instead sought happiness and fulfillment through their own efforts. The pursuit of utopianism in the 1960s transformed itself in the 1970s into an obsessive search for "personal growth." In neither decade did we find what we were looking for. Instead, as a society, we became increasingly obsessed with personal comfort, emotional satisfaction and selfish pursuits. As a society, we became increasingly desensitized towards the welfare of our communities and humanity as a whole (Lasch, 1991).

According to research data, since the 1970s non-diagnosable levels of narcissism among college students have steadily risen. A large-scale epidemiologic study suggests that young adults are much more likely than older adults to be diagnosed with narcissistic personality disorder (Dingfelder, 2011). According to Dr. Jean M. Twenge, author of *Generation Me* (2006) and *The Narcissism Epidemic* (2010), narcissism is on the rise, especially with the twenty-something generation. Dr. Twenge suggested that the "millennial" generation, those who were born roughly between 1982 and 1989, may feel more entitlement and self-centeredness than previous generations. Dr. Twenge's findings were based on the largest intergenerational research study ever conducted. The study analyzed data that included surveys of 1.3 million young people, some dating back to the 1920s. Her research demonstrated a progressive generational trend in self-esteem, assertiveness, self-importance and high expectations, all of which are associated with narcissism.

According to Dr. Nathan Dewall's 2011 research, late adolescents and college students are demonstrating more narcissistic traits than in previous generations. In a study conducted by him and his colleagues, it was revealed that song lyrics from 1980 to 2007 had a distinct trend toward narcissistic content (Dewall, Pond, Campbell, Twenge 2011). Using a computer analysis of three decades of hit songs, the research team found a statistically significant trend toward narcissistic lyrics in popular music. To illustrate, the words "I" and "me" appear more frequently, while words like "we" and "us" declined. The research revealed that songs in the 1980s were more likely to emphasize togetherness, harmony and love, while songs in the last decade were distinctly written about what an individual wants and how they have been disappointed or wronged. Today's songs, according to this study, are more likely to be about one very important and loved person: the singer or the song writer.

The words "narcissistic" and "narcissism" are typically used to describe a person who is excessively absorbed and fascinated with himself and is overly concerned about his outward appearance, qualities and achievements. It is also used to describe an individual who demonstrates over-the-top self-admiration, self-love, self-centeredness, egocentrism, smugness and arrogance. According to Eleanor Payson, author of *The Wizard of Oz and Other Narcissists* (2002),

"The word narcissism in its most fundamental
sense means a tendency to self-worship"
(p. 5).

The origins of the word can be traced back to the Greek myth of Narcissus and Echo. Narcissus was the handsome and very charming son of the river god, Cephissus. Because of his exquisite good looks, charm, and alluring sex appeal, all of the young women in his fabled community desperately sought his attention. Narcissus would reject each and every young woman that fell in love with him. One of the unfortunate young women who was mesmerized by Narcissus' handsome looks and appealing charm was a young woman named Echo. As with the other women, Narcissus spurned her advances and refused to accept her love. As a result of Echo's humiliating rejection, as well as complaints by the other aggrieved young women, the avenging goddess Nemesis, passed judgment on Narcissus, cursing him to neither experience love nor the return of affection. He was also cursed to fall hopelessly in love with an image of himself. This curse would cause him to feel rejection, sadness, emptiness and loneliness, all of which the women he rejected felt. Because of the curse, Narcissus would never be able to experience love of anyone, including himself.

One day, Narcissus knelt down to take a drink from a pool of water and caught sight of his own reflection. Not knowing that this was a mirror image of himself, he fell immediately and completely in love with the reflected image of his beautiful face. Narcissus was mesmerized by his likeness and could not pull himself away from it. He spent days and nights staring at the image, hoping that he would feel or experience a union or loving connection with it. There he would remain until he died slowly of starvation. Poor Narcissus died while trying to obtain the love of the one person he was completely unable to love – himself. Because of Narcissus' obsession with himself, he would never experience true and real intimacy. Narcissus would spend the rest of his life unsuccessfully trying to obtain a love that could never be. Narcissus was the original narcissist.

Healthy Narcissism

Prior to discussing the narcissistic personality disorder and its subtypes, it is important to first mention that narcissistic traits exist on a continuum. On one end of the continuum would lie the mildest narcissists, on the other, the most severe. The psychologically healthy "narcissist" would value and seek recognition, praise, and affirmation while being confident, moderately boastful and assertive in the pursuit of their goals. Healthy narcissists do not denigrate others or make them feel bad about not being as gifted, talented or motivated as them. They would be perceived as confident and boastful, while also seeming humble, sensitive and empathetic. They simply enjoy feeling important, valued and recognized while not wanting or needing to hurt or harm anyone in the process. Healthy narcissists are also aware of their robust confidence and self-promoting behaviors. According to Simon Crompton, author of *All About Me: Loving a Narcissist* (2008),

"Some…make a distinction between "healthy narcissism" and "unhealthy narcissism"…the healthy narcissist being someone who has a real sense of self-esteem that can enable them to leave their imprint on the world, but who can also share in the emotional life of others. It could be successfully argued that some level of narcissism is healthy"
(p. 37).

We all know someone, whether it be a friend, sibling, co-worker, friend, etc., who is consistently comfortable in a role of "the life of the party," the "know-it-all" or the talented and/or comfortable performer. As much as these individuals are motivated to flaunt their talent and fulfill their own personal needs, they also desire to care, love and respect others. As much as these individuals are motivated to fulfill their own personal needs they also desire to care for, love and respect others. The CSVs for these individuals would be a (+1) to a (+2). To be fair, healthy narcissists shouldn't even be called narcissists, since the term has definite negative connotations.

Benign or Mild Narcissism

Benign or mild narcissists are represented on the continuum of self as a CSV of (+3). They are able to participate in and sustain healthy relationships, although they are tilted slightly toward the self-centered side. They are slightly self-obsessed and can be unintentionally mildly annoying to others. Traits of a benign or mild narcissist would include an active tendency to seek praise, affirmation and recognition for their unique personality, talents, skill sets, or contributions. They may be periodically self-consumed, over-the-top confident, and mildly entitled. These individuals are aware of their self-indulgences, but are able to moderate them, especially if they have upset or offended someone, or if they are criticized for their narcissistic behavior. Seldom do their narcissistic tendencies result in harm. Although benign narcissists are periodically carried away with themselves, they have the ability to be aware of these tendencies and, when necessary, are able to control or modulate them. Additionally, they do not become angered or hostile when confronted about them.

Benign or mild narcissism could be a product of immaturity, as younger adults are often more self-centered and self-obsessed than their older and wiser counterparts. Younger adults are still learning about social norms and age- appropriate behavior. They simply do not yet have the life experience to understand the negative aspects or consequences of their narcissistic tendencies.

Benign narcissists may be well-liked and successful in their careers, as they work very hard to get noticed while going the extra mile to make sure people appreciate and take note of their skill sets. Since they are capable of mild to moderate levels of empathy and mutuality in their relationships, they are not experienced as characteristically harmful or hurtful. Their benign pursuit of attention and recognition combined with a tendency to seek the spotlight is likely to endear them to their friends. They are often appreciated and valued for their affable, charming, funny and confident natures. Loving center stage and seeking recognition, these individuals are also valued for their entertainment value. After all, in our culture, being confident and self-assured are admired personality traits.

Moderate Narcissism

Although moderate narcissists may be exasperating and challenging, they do not qualify for a narcissistic personality disorder (NPD) diagnosis. They exist in the "darker" area on the narcissistic continuum – between annoying/bothersome and pathological. According to the continuum of self theory, moderate narcissists have a CSV of (+4), which means they are able to participate in relationships where they are only able to reciprocate with low levels of love, respect and caring.

In a relationship, moderate narcissists are exhausting, as they require constant attention, affirmation, and validation. Unlike those with a diagnosable narcissistic personality disorder, they have some insight and control over their narcissistic traits. Many of us know and even love these narcissists; they are our friends, family members or loved ones who consistently expend a great deal of energy making sure we know of their value, importance, uniqueness, etc. They thrive on any positive attention and recognition. They excessively value and are consequently motivated to seek admiration, attention, status, understanding and support.

Moderate narcissists wear their self-value on their sleeves. They are prone to bragging about their worth, talent and successes, sometimes to the annoyance of others. Like benign narcissists, they are often the life of the party, the resident expert, know-it-all, comedian or entertainer. They like to announce their accomplishments and skills, as well as their ability to make things happen for others. Unlike benign narcissists, they do not always know when to stop their attention-seeking or bothersome narcissistic behaviors.

Unlike the individual who has been diagnosed with narcissistic personality disorder, the moderately narcissistic person is capable, albeit in a limited fashion, of being empathetic and unconditionally giving in their relationships. They are also capable of participating in and sustaining lower-level reciprocal and mutual relationships. The value of sharing and giving is not lost on them. Even though they struggle with regulating their narcissistic traits, they can be loyal friends; just ones who are much more tilted on the "me" side than the "you." Moderate narcissists are able of meeting some, but not most, of their loved ones' emotional and personal needs. When necessary or demanded, they are able to suspend their self-centered, self-obsessed and selfish ways. They are capable of benefitting from therapy, as they are able to take limited responsibility for their behaviors and the treatment of their partner.

Moderate narcissists thrive in careers in which they can be the center of attention, perform, and openly showcase their talents, abilities and successes. Their professional successes can, in fact, be enhanced by their tendency to seek success while making sure everyone is aware of it. Careers such as music, acting, academia, business management, and politics are not only appealing to them, but naturally fit their personality. Professions that require a public demonstration of one's skills and abilities will be naturally enticing to a moderate-level narcissist.

Moderate narcissists are typically neither malicious nor intentionally harmful in their pursuit of recognition and praise. Due to their capacity for personal insight, albeit limited, they are able to control or modulate certain elements of their narcissism. Unlike a person with true narcissistic personality disorder, they are able to respond to constructive criticism without reflexively striking back or hurting the person giving it to them. Moderate narcissists do not respond to constructive feedback or criticism with reflexive anger, rage or humiliation (narcissistic injury). And when their narcissism injures others, they are able to experience limited amounts of remorse and empathy for those they unintentionally affected. Nonetheless, moderate narcissists walk a fine line between robust self-confidence, arrogance, entitlement and egotism and a more pathological and harmful form of narcissism – narcissistic personality disorder.

Narcissistic Personality Disorder (NPD)

"Unrestrained self-love" is this author's favorite simple definition of narcissistic personality disorder (NPD). As with other personality disorders, NPD individuals are generally unaware of and oblivious to their psychological disorder. Individuals diagnosed with NPD are considered pathologically selfish, self-absorbed, grandiose and egotistic. They are motivated by a long-standing and insatiable desire for admiration, praise, and validation. The NPDs constant need for affirmation, validation and attention, often wears their partner down, as there can never be enough compliments and affirmation to make them feel good enough. As metaphorical sponges, they are able to soak up praise and compliments, but, because of their psychologically porous (underdeveloped) nature, they cannot hold on to them.

NPDs are compelled to direct, correct or continually remind others how to do things correctly. They tend to monopolize conversations while presenting themselves as the resident expert at many things, especially the subject at hand. They are adept at turning conversations around to what they know and their own related experiences. As self-proclaimed experts, they believe and behave as if they are morally and intellectually superior to others. They tend to turn conversations into either a lecture or presentation in which they are compelled to correct others while sharing their insight and accomplishments. NPDs are not shy about bragging about their supposed wealth of knowledge and their dramatic climb to success. Unbeknownst to them, their proclamations about greatness and success are not always grounded in reality.

Narcissistic personality disorder, like the other two emotional manipulation personality disorders, is represented on the continuum of self as a (+5) CSV. This "severe" CSV is indicative of a self-orientation that is almost completely focused on the needs of one's self at the exclusion of the LRC needs of others. According to the authors of the DSM-IV-TR™, 1% of the US population suffers from narcissistic personality disorder and 50-75% are men. Because individuals with a personality disorder tend either to deny it or are oblivious to it, gathering data about NPD is at best challenging. Since most statistics are compiled by self-report data, it is likely that the DSM statistics far under-represent the actual prevalence of NPD.

According to the DSM-IV-TR™, narcissistic personality disorder is categorized as an Axis II mental condition/disorder. The DSM utilizes a multi-axial assessment and diagnosis system to categorize all mental conditions. The Axis I category is reserved for clinical, developmental and learning disorders. Typical Axis I disorders include major depression, attention deficit hyperactivity disorder, schizophrenia, generalized anxiety disorder, addiction disorders and many more, all of which are characterized by periods of illness and remission and are typically responsive to medical and/or psychological treatment. Most mental health or mental illness disorders are classified in the Axis I category.

Axis II disorders, on the other hand, include mental health disorders or mental illnesses that are long-standing, ongoing, persistent and not typically amenable and receptive to treatment. These disorders typically take shape and start to appear in adolescence, persisting throughout a person's lifetime. Common Axis II disorders include intellectual disabilities, i.e., developmental disabilities and personality disorders, *which include the three emotional manipulation personality disorders.* It should be noted that to receive a DSM diagnosis, a qualified diagnostician using the required diagnostic protocol must match the client's symptoms and degree of pathology to a specific number of criteria, as listed in the DSM-IV-TR™. Only experienced, trained and qualified mental health professionals can make actual diagnoses. In most states, such clinicians include psychiatrists, psychologists, and licensed and qualified master's level clinicians.

A Pattern of Grandiosity

According to the DSM, narcissistic personality disorder is understood as: "A pervasive pattern of grandiosity (in fantasy or behavior), need for admiration, and lack of empathy, beginning by early adulthood and present in a variety of contexts, as indicated by five (or more) of the following:

- Has a grandiose sense of self-importance (e.g., exaggerates achievements and talents, expects to be recognized as superior without commensurate achievements)

- Is preoccupied with fantasies of unlimited success, power, brilliance, beauty, or ideal love

- Believes that he or she is "special" and unique and can only be understood by, or should associate with, other special or high status people (or institutions)

- Requires excessive admiration

- Has a sense of entitlement, i.e., unreasonable expectations of especially favorable treatment or automatic compliance with his or her expectations

- Is interpersonally exploitative, i.e., takes advantage of others to achieve his or her own ends

- Lacks empathy: is unwilling to recognize or identify with the feelings and needs of others

- Is often envious of others or believes that others are envious of him or her

- Shows arrogant, haughty behaviors or attitudes"(American Psychiatric Publishing, 2000)

Since NPD individuals carry a heavy unconscious burden of shame and deep feelings of inadequacy, they compensate through an obsession with power and status. They are excessively proud and fixated on their own achievements and appearances. Their vanity, whether it is for their physical or personality attributes, often rises to the level of an obsession. As a result of their inflated self-appraisal and their consequent need to show others their positive qualities and contributions, they are typically experienced as arrogant and conceited.

Individuals diagnosed with narcissistic personality disorders are incapable of sustaining relationships that are mutual and reciprocal. They have a limited capacity for empathy and sensitivity to others, especially when they feel in competition or threatened. Additionally, individuals with NPD are generous to others only when personal gain is imminent. Their strings-attached approach to relationships exemplifies their self-serving nature. Their selfish interpersonal exchanges and one-sided relationships are experienced as aggravating and offensive to anyone except a codependent/an individual with a CSV (-5).

As a direct result of their underdeveloped self-concept and very low levels of self-esteem (which they are oblivious to), NPDs usually over-react to their mistakes or perceived flaws. They are acutely sensitive about making errors or the possibility that they may be criticized or judged. Even when the comments are constructive or benign, they react as if someone told them they are "bad" or "stupid." They internalize the constructive criticism as if the critic is purposefully and maliciously trying to embarrass them or to prove to others that they are "wrong" or "bad." The narcissist's fragile self-esteem simply cannot accommodate feeling mistaken or humiliated. They counter almost instantaneously with anger and contempt for the "judgmental" person. Instead of processing the value of the critical feedback, they react smugly and angrily – sometimes even aggressively. Alternatively, they may shut down emotionally, sulk, and/or behave passive-aggressively.

Any perceived threat to a narcissist's self-esteem or self-worth is referred to as a narcissistic injury. NPDs often punish the perpetrators of the narcissistic injury, be they friends, loved ones or family members. It is not that they intend to hurt a person who triggers their narcissistic injury. Rather, the aggravated anger, reflexive indignation and resentment that accompanies a narcissistic injury is more of a product of very low self-esteem and self-loathing, of which they are largely unaware. NPDs aggressive and incensed reaction to the narcissistic injury is considered "narcissistic rage." Once enraged, the NPD is typically unable to stop or control their destructive behavior. Because the narcissistic personality disordered individual is unaware and unable to take responsibility for their harmful reactions, they are quick to blame others for "starting it." NPDs rarely apologize for their wrong-doings except when they are cornered and imminent gain may result from an act of contrition.

Full-blown NPDs are experienced as pretentious and arrogant. They tend to brag, embellish and proclaim their unique talents. As grandiose individuals who assert themselves as an expert in most matters, they believe and behave as if they are morally and intellectually superior to others. NPDs are compelled to remind others of their successful pursuit of glory and prestige. To maintain their distorted feelings of superiority, they are compelled to degrade, diminish or discredit the achievements of others. To that end, they may even terminate a long-standing relationship if they feel threatened or hindered in their pursuit of recognition.

As a result of their unreasonable expectations and over-inflated ego, the NPDs believe they should automatically receive preferential treatment and automatic compliance with any request or desire. From the NPD's point of view, she naturally should always come first. The entitled NPDs are the ones that cut in a long line or insist they get a table at a restaurant immediately, despite the annoyance of others who have waited equally long. One NPD I knew, took his disabled parent's handicapped parking permit and shamelessly used it himself to obtain preferential parking.

NARCISSISTIC PERSONALITY SUBTYPES

Narcissistic personality disorder can be further categorized into subtypes. While outward characteristics may vary, the internal narcissistic psychological dynamics are similar.

Overt Narcissism

Overt Narcissism is the "garden variety" form of narcissistic personality disorder. It is an unapologetic and obvious expression of NPD. These individuals lead with an up-front, in your face form of grandiosity, entitlement, self-absorption and conceit. Outwardly, they are confident, brash and charismatic, often seeking or demanding the spotlight, relishing any opportunities that can garner them attention and admiration. Overt narcissism and a narcissistic personality disorder, as defined by the DSM-IV-TR™, are the same.

Covert Narcissism

Covert narcissists are masters of disguise – successful actors, humanitarians, politicians, clergy members, and even psychotherapists who are beloved and appreciated, but are secretly selfish, calculating, controlling, angry and vindictive. Covert narcissists create an illusion of selflessness while gaining from their elevated status. Although they share similar basic traits with the overt narcissist, i.e., the need for attention, affirmation, approval and recognition, they are stealthier about hiding their selfish and egocentric motives. Unlike the overt narcissist who parades his narcissism for all to see, the covert narcissist furtively hides his real motives and identity. These narcissists are able to trick others into believing they are honest, altruistic and empathetic individuals. They are successful at pretending to be a more likable version of themselves, knowing that if their true identity was uncovered, they would not be able to maintain the respect, status and prestige that they have so furtively garnered.

A common variation of the covert narcissist is a parent who expends an inordinate amount of time and energy taking care of all aspects of their children. These individuals are admired and held in high regard for what appears to be their tireless and dedicated efforts to be all things at all times for their child. Their frequent complaints about the personal and emotional costs of their sacrifice are really manipulative ploys orchestrated for attention and praise. Although to the outside world they seem like an unconditionally giving and generous parent, in reality, all of their actions are motivated by their insatiable need for recognition, admiration and respect. The child's emotional needs are ultimately secondary to their own narcissistic requirement for validation, affirmation and attention. Unfortunately, the only person who has a bird's eye view of this covert narcissist's real intentions is their child. Like all other covert narcissists, close friends and family members are privy to their more shameful and hidden agenda.

> **A [covert narcissist] displays a persona that allows him to cover and disguise the grandiose needs by displaying an identity of helper, humanitarian, expert professional, rebel without a cause, misunderstood artist, or hermit. This persona allows the narcissist to gain attention, status, and power through what he is doing and what he is connected to, rather than attempt to command a truly solo role in the spotlight. In fact, the covert narcissist may at times outwardly show a disdain of the spotlight with an aloof and indifferent demeanor.**

(Payson, 2002)

Compared to overt narcissists, covert narcissists are more reserved and composed. By not advertising their deeper narcissistic values and motives, they are able to achieve their goals, while protecting their innermost insecurities and vulnerabilities. Unlike overt narcissists, they expend a great deal of psychological energy containing or hiding their callous, indifferent, and manipulative inner selves. Even though covert narcissists have repressed the full scope and magnitude of their personality disorder, on a semi-conscious level, they are aware that their fantasies are embarrassing and unacceptable.

Because covert narcissists are able to create and maintain a facade of altruism and unconditional positive regard, they are able to function in positions that are traditionally not attractive to narcissists, e.g., clergy, teachers, politicians, psychotherapists and others. Even though they are able to replicate the known characteristics of these positions, they are often deeply insecure and secretive about their lack of knowledge or inability to perform the most essential tasks. For example, a covert narcissist who is a psychotherapist will have mastered the stereotypical career-specific, idiosyncratic behavior patterns such as reflective listening, supporting and accepting feedback, and gestures that mimic unconditional acceptance. However, this psychotherapist will be deficient in the most critical area of the job. Although they attempt to demonstrate honesty, sympathy and empathy with their clients, they ultimately fall short. They are simply unable to master the key elements of the position, as they are inherently judgmental, controlling and emotionally aloof. These therapists often become agitated at their clients when challenged or questioned. Clients who do not let them control the process will often trigger a narcissistic injury.

Productive Narcissism

Michael Maccoby, a noted anthropologist and psychoanalyst, coined the term "productive narcissist." According to his articles and books on the subject, productive narcissists are extraordinarily useful and even a necessary manifestation of NPD. Although similar to overt narcissists, productive narcissists are responsible for society's greatest achievements. Because of their fervent desire to make the world a better place, they task themselves with the responsibility to come up with important inventions, achievements and contributions to humanity. They are supremely gifted and creative intellectuals, inventors, business leaders, politicians, etc., who find great meaning in making the world a better place, and by leaving behind a lasting legacy. Andrew Carnegie, John D. Rockefeller, Thomas Edison and Henry Ford are examples of this subcategory of narcissism.

These narcissists are driven by an unwavering passion to achieve and build great things, not for themselves, for the betterment of mankind. Similar to overt and covert narcissists, productive narcissists are hyper-sensitive to criticism, exhibiting over-competitive, grandiose, isolated and pompous tendencies. As a direct result of being recognized and praised for their profound intellectual and creative gifts, they actually come close to obtaining their grandiose ideals and fantasies. Their successes give them the opportunity to bypass the limitations which entangle many narcissists. It is not that they are more oriented towards the needs of others than other narcissists; rather, they are completely consumed by their quest to make a difference. Their obsession to contribute to the world in which they live is still a narcissistic process, as it is ultimately motivated by their tireless pursuit to convince themselves of their greatness.

Even with all their abilities, productive narcissists are prone to self-destruction. With their successes, they start to believe in their grandiose fantasies and feelings of invulnerability. Consumed by their success and believing they are invincible, they listen less to advice or words of caution. Over time, increasing levels of grandiosity lead them to take unnecessary risks and be increasingly careless. As they lose perspective on their human limitations and start to identify with their elaborate ambitions, they start to behave as if they are beyond reproach and unaccountable for their mistakes or wrongdoings. Their entitlement, grandiosity and flagrant disregard for rules and laws eventually lead them to catastrophe. Fallen productive narcissists are often successful at redemption since the very same gifts that brought them to their creative and productive apex can be utilized to get them back on track with their fantasies of greatness.

Malignant Narcissism

In 1984, Dr. Otto Kernberg, a Cornell University psychoanalyst, coined the diagnostic term "malignant narcissism." Kernberg believed that there is a narcissism continuum, with NPD at the low end, and malignant narcissism with psychopathic features at the high end. Malignant narcissism appears to be a hybrid of NPD, as it is a combination of four pathological extremes: narcissism, psychopathy, sadism and paranoia. Even with the other forms of psychopathology, they are still distinctly narcissistic as they demonstrate most narcissistic traits/symptoms. The difference, though, is that malignant narcissists are able to force their grandiose fantasies onto others.

Like NPDs, they are entitled and grandiose. However, malignant narcissists take it to a more extreme level because they believe they have a special destiny in life. By believing in their special status or destiny, their extreme sense of entitlement and grandiosity in their relationships is reinforced. They are outwardly selfish and unapologetic, while also feeling compelled to direct the lives around them. They are often suspicious of others, especially those who could remove them from their position of power. They are belligerent and scheming, while manipulatively casting themselves as the injured party. They often rise to influence by claiming they are victims of oppression. As a direct result of their beguiling charm and calculating nature, they are able to sympathetically rally support for their cause. With legions of dedicated followers, they are able to lead and inspire rebellions, which in turn secure their leadership and power structure.

Because malignant narcissists are fundamentally insecure and paranoid in their relationships, they counter by maintaining complete and total control of others. With a rise to power through popular support, they believe there is a mandate for them to maintain power and strict control over their legions of followers. Once they have achieved control, they will do almost anything to maintain it, including rape, murder, and even genocide. As a direct result of their paranoid and psychopathic tendencies, they challenge, defy, demean and even murder anyone who is either an authority figure or has the power to hurt them. Examples of malignant narcissists include Adolph Hitler, Joseph Stalin, Muammar Gaddafi and Saddam Hussein.

Malignant narcissists are known to be emotionally, physically and/ or sexually abusive and will purposely and maliciously harm others. Their cruel and harmful treatment of others is reinforced by their need to maintain power, control, and a sense of superiority over others. Although they seem similar to psychopaths or those diagnosed with an antisocial personality disorder, they are different in that they can internalize right and wrong, form meaningful personal and social relationships and rationalize their actions as a desire to advance society. They may be loyal in relationships, but because of their paranoia, may hurt or harm those who pledge loyalty to them.

Addiction-Induced Narcissism

Individuals who are addicted to a drug or a behavior (a process addiction) often behave in narcissistic and self-serving ways. Although they do not have a specific personality disorder, their pursuit and use of their drug of choice, often is expressed in pathological narcissistic behaviors/traits. Only after a sustained period of recovery is it possible to determine if an addict can also be diagnosed with NPD. If the addict does not have NPD, his NPD symptoms will abate. If the recovering addict maintains his narcissistic symptomatology, then he likely has a co-occurring narcissistic personality disorder.

CHAPTER 12

Borderline Personality Disorder (BPD)

The American Psychiatric Association estimates that 2% of the American population, approximately six million people, is affected by Borderline Personality Disorder (DSM-IV-TR™). According to a SAMHSA's (The Substance Abuse and Mental Health Services Administration) report entitled, "The Report to Congress on Borderline Personality Disorder,"

"an estimated 18 million Americans will develop borderline personality disorder (BPD) in their lifetimes, with symptoms commonly emerging during early adolescence and adulthood"

(SAMHSA, 2011).

BPD is more common than other recognized mental illnesses, such as schizophrenia and bipolar disorder (Nordqvist, 2012). It is common among adolescents and young adults, with the highest rates occurring between the ages of 18 and 35 (Oliver, 2012). Self-injuring behaviors that are symptomatic of this disorder can emerge as young as ages 10-12 (SAMHSA, 2011). Until recently, it was believed to be more prevalent in females. However, recent research by the National Institute of Mental Health (NIMH) indicates that BPD is equally distributed between the sexes (Grant et al, 2008). The prevalence of BPD in the clinical setting is considerably higher than in the general population, at an estimated 10 percent of outpatient clinics and 15-20 percent or more of inpatient settings (Swartz et al., 1990).

Borderline personality disorder is considered the most self-destructive and unstable of all mental illnesses/disorders. BPDs exhibit various self-destructive patterns, such as self-mutilation, chemical dependency, eating disorders and suicide attempts. "Borderlines are the patients psychologists fear most. As many as 75% hurt themselves, and approximately 10% commit suicide – an extraordinarily high suicide rate (by comparison, the suicide rate for mood disorders is about 6%)" (Cloud, 2009). According to the aforementioned SAMHSA report on BPD:

BPD carries an 8-10 percent rate of death by suicide, which is 50 times greater than in the general population. More than 70 percent of individuals with BPD will attempt suicide at least once. Suicide attempts tend to peak when consumers are in their 20s and 30s, though suicidality is not by any means restricted to these age groups. In addition, the estimated rate of self-harm (i.e., self-destructive behaviors such as cutting or other self-injury with no suicidal intent) is as high as 60-80 percent of those with the diagnosis.
(SAMHSA, 2010, p. 20)

The diagnostic term, borderline personality disorder (BPD), was officially recognized with the 1980 publication of the DSM-III. At that time, the term borderline was thought to describe a person who was on the "border" between psychosis and neurosis. As a direct result of advances in the mental health and psychiatric fields, combined with cultural and societal advances, some diagnostic terms eventually lost their descriptive value. BPD is one such example. To illustrate, the term "neurotic" is a Freudian term that is rarely used today in the mental health field. Terms like "neurotic" and other psychoanalytic terms of the late 19th and early 20th centuries ultimately became obsolete. Moreover, it's no longer believed that BPDs struggle with psychosis as their primary symptom. Currently, there are rumblings in the mental health field about the negative implications of the BPD term itself, as many consider it misleading, stigmatizing and fraught with negative associations. According to Valerie Porr (2001), the President of the Treatment and Research Advancement Association for Personality Disorders:

Borderline personality disorder may be among the most stigmatized of mental disorders. It is often undiagnosed, misdiagnosed, or treated inappropriately. Clinicians may limit the number of BPD patients in their practice or drop them as 'treatment resistant.'

At present, there are calls to de-stigmatize the diagnostic term by renaming it something that has a more appropriate descriptive value, e.g., "emotional dysregulation disorder" or "emotional regulation disorder."

Borderline personality disorder is characterized by instability in mood, self-image, thought processes and personal relationships. When unable to regulate their emotions or mood, borderlines engage in wild, reckless and out-of-control behaviors, i.e., dangerous sexual liaisons, drug abuse, gambling, spending sprees or eating binges. Prominent characteristics of mood dysregulation include rapidly fluctuating mood swings with periods of intense depression, irritability and/or anxiety, which can last a few hours to a few days. Borderlines become overwhelmed and incapacitated by the intensity of their emotions, whether it is joy and elation or depression, anxiety or rage. They are unable to regulate or control these intense emotions. A common term used to describe a BPD's struggles in controlling their emotions is emotional dysregulation. It aptly describes the borderline's inability to effectively manage or regulate their powerful emotions. When upset, they experience a flurry of intense emotions, distorted and dangerous thought processes, and destructive mood swings, which threaten the safety of others, as well as themselves.

The DSM-IV-TR™ (2000) Diagnostic Criteria for borderline personality disorder is:

A pervasive pattern of instability related to interpersonal relationships, self-image and affects, and marked impulsivity beginning by early adulthood and are present in a variety of contexts, as indicated by five (or more) of the following:

- Frantic efforts to avoid real or imagined abandonment.

- A pattern of unstable and intense interpersonal relationships characterized by alternating between extremes of idealization and devaluation.

- Identity disturbance: Markedly and persistently unstable self-image or sense of self.

- Impulsivity in at least two areas that are potentially self-damaging (e.g., spending, sex, substance abuse, reckless driving, binge eating).

- Recurrent suicidal behavior, gestures or threats, or self-mutilating behavior.

- Affective (emotional) instability due to a marked reactivity of mood, e.g., intense episodic dysphoria (intense feelings of depression, discontent and, in some cases, indifference), irritability or anxiety, usually lasting a few hours and only rarely more than a few days.

- Chronic feelings of emptiness.

- Inappropriate, intense anger or difficulty controlling anger (e.g., frequent displays of temper, constant anger, recurrent physical fights).

- Transient, stress-related or paranoid thoughts and severe dissociative symptoms.

Borderline personality disorder is expressed on the continuum of self as a CSV of (+5). This love/hate or rigidly dichotomous approach to relationships is entirely a narcissistic process, as the direction of the relationship is always determined by the BPD's feelings at any given moment. Unlike the individual with a narcissistic personality disorder, BPDs seem to demonstrate a capacity and a willingness to be genuinely empathetic, sensitive, generous and sacrificial. However, those positive attributes are not without the proverbial "strings attached;" when the BPD explodes with vindictive rage, all that they said or gave to their loved one may be taken away in one fell swoop of aggravated aggression.

Life in Extremes: Love/Hate

BPDs experience the world in extremes: black-and-white or all-or-nothing. When they are happy, the world is a beautiful and perfect place. The joy that borderlines experience is as perfect as any person's joy can be. On the other hand, BPDs reflexively experience reckless rage, paranoia and feelings of hopelessness when they perceive that they are being rejected or abandoned. Their swing into red-hot, out-of-control fury brings them to the brink of harming themselves or others. In extreme circumstances of depression, agitation or rage, the borderline may spontaneously behave violently and lethally – to self and/or others. As mentioned previously, BPD carries the highest risk of suicide of all the mental disorders. Their irresponsible disregard for the safety and welfare of themselves or others creates a wide swath of destruction that leaves permanent marks on all that are affected.

BPDs typically don't intend to cause harm to anyone including themselves, but their reflexive emotional rampages create a form of temporary insanity. During moments of a complete emotional meltdown, their thought processes, insight into their emotional state and abilities to make sound and rational decisions become severely impaired. They will put themselves and loved ones in harm's way because of an irrational and uncontrollable wave of hatred, rage and paranoia, however brief. BPDs may cause injury to themselves or others, not due to a lack of love, but because in that moment, they have been triggered to experience the wrath and rage connected to repressed (unconscious) memories of their abusive, neglectful and traumatic childhood.

Unless their romantic partner is a codependent (CSV of -5), BPDs are rarely capable of sustaining stable long-term relationships. Their romantic relationships begin quickly, intensely, and with a great deal of excitement, euphoria and sexual chemistry. Their volatile emotions move in one of two directions: love and adoration or hatred and destruction. Because the borderline has had little to no experience in healthy and stable relationships, the euphoric "perfect love" feelings that occur in the beginning of the relationship are neither realistic nor lasting. A BPD's early euphoric "love" experience is transient though, as their psychological fragility leads them to an eventual emotional "crash and burn." This black-and-white approach to their romances creates a teeter totter of extreme behavior, either showering their partner with love and kindness or raging at them with disgust and violence. Their all-or-nothing or love/hate processing of relationships places an impossible burden on the partner.[13]

Abandonment: The Core Issue

The cornerstone of a BPD's thought process is a preoccupation with real or imagined abandonment, which they frantically try to avoid. Depending on the borderline's understanding and perception of the status of their relationship, they typically vacillate between love and trust and hatred and paranoid suspicion. At one moment they may seem calm and serene and deeply in love with their partner, but at the next, they may be triggered by an event that leads them to *feel* criticized or abandoned, which irrationally provokes an outburst of harmful aggressive rage. The perception of impending separation or rejection can lead to profound changes in the manner in which they think about themselves and others as well as their emotional stability and behavior. Whether real or imagined, a thought or reminder that they could be rejected or abandoned causes them to strike back at their romantic partner with rage and aggressive hostility.

A mistaken comment, a benign disagreement, or an expression perceived as disappointing can quickly transform their loving feelings toward their "soul mate" into a raging retribution against an enemy.

Individuals with BPD are chronically unsure about their lives, whether it is with their family, personal relationships, work or future aspirations. They also experience persistent uncertain and insecure thoughts and feelings about their self-image, long-term goals, friendships and values. They often suffer from chronic boredom or feelings of emptiness. According to Marsha Linehan, one of the world's leading experts on BPD, "Borderline individuals are the psychological equivalent of third-degree-burn patients. They simply have, so to speak, no emotional skin. Even the slightest touch or movement can create immense suffering" (Linehan, 1993). According to Kreisman and Straus, the authors of *I Hate You, Don't Leave Me: Understanding the Borderline Personality,*

---

[13] Except for a (-5) CSV codependent, who, by virtue of their psychopathology, is able to manage the destructive nature of the BPD.

"A borderline suffers from a kind of 'emotional hemophilia;' she lacks the clotting mechanism needed to moderate her spurts of feeling. Prick the delicate 'skin' of a borderline, and she will emotionally bleed to death"

(p. 12).

The borderline's fear of abandonment and rejection creates a self-fulfilling prophecy, which is defined by businessdictionary.com as "any positive or negative expectation about circumstances, events, or people that may affect a person's behavior toward them in a manner that causes those expectations to be fulfilled." In order to feel safe and secure, thereby allaying their fear of abandonment, they form romantic relationships quickly and intensely. Through a quickly developed emotional and sexual union, they are temporarily shielded from terrifying feelings of loneliness and worthlessness. These quickly-formed attachments can only temporarily relieve or decrease their anxiety and fears of abandonment as the borderline is profoundly psychologically damaged.

In relationships, BPDs are often clingy, insecure and needy as they seek frequent reassurances of their value and worthiness. When all is well, they experience and relish a bliss-like euphoria. However, when triggered by benign or real threats of abandonment, they quickly devolve into a state of fear and insecurity, which triggers them to strike back, push away from or break up with their seemingly offending partner. When they react with harmful and damaging retribution, typically if their partner is not codependent, they will have caused the relationship to fail, creating the very situation they fear most: abandonment. If the partner happens to be codependent, a cycle of love, destruction and reconciliation will be repeated.

Perhaps the most famous celebrity who is suspected to have borderline personality disorder is Marilyn Monroe. Marilyn, whose birth name was Norma Jean Mortenson, was repeatedly traumatized early in her life; she experienced deprivation, neglect and emotional, physical and sexual abuse. According to IMDB.com, Marilyn was almost smothered to death by her mother at age two, nearly raped at six, and raped at age 11. Her mother, a paranoid schizophrenic, was in and out of mental hospitals throughout her childhood. She experienced little to no stability in childhood, growing up in the homes of relatives, foster homes and in orphanages. Marilyn dropped out of school at age 15. To escape the abuse at an orphanage, she married her high school boyfriend at age 16.

Marilyn suffered from chronic loneliness. Later in life, she tried to fill her deep emptiness and sought an identity through relationships with strong, caretaking men who she hoped would protect her and make her feel safe and loved. While needing and depending on these men, she was also constantly obsessed that they would abandon her. Her relationships with men could never fulfill her deep emotional needs, as she was just too psychologically damaged. Despite her beauty and fame, she could not escape experiencing loneliness and fear of abandonment, which she buried deep inside of her. Elton John and Bernie Taupin immortalized Marilyn's precarious emotional battle with relationships in the song, *Candle in the Wind*. (John, E. & Taupin, B., 1973)

Seems to me you lived your life
like a candle in the wind
Never knowing who to cling to
when the rain set in

Borderline personality disorder made national news in July of 2011 when Brandon Marshall, a National Football League wide receiver, openly announced that he had been diagnosed with BPD and was seeking treatment for it. Marshall's disclosure came on the heels of Dr. Marsha Linehan's revelation in June of 2011 that she, the pioneer of dialectical behavior therapy for BPD, also lived with the condition. As a result of these two high-profile individuals as well as the various movements and initiatives to teach the public about BPD, the stigma against this mental health disorder is slowly changing.

CHAPTER 13
Antisocial Personality Disorder (ASPD)

Of all the emotional manipulators (and personality disorders), the antisocial personality disordered individuals are by far the most insidious, manipulative and harmful. For that matter, they are the most narcissistic of the emotional manipulator disorders. Antisocial personality disorder, according to the DSM-IV-TR™, is characterized by a pervasive pattern of disregard for, and violation of, the rights of others that begins in childhood or early adolescence and continues into adulthood.

ASPDs possess distorted and destructive patterns of thinking, perceiving and relating to others. They lack empathy, demonstrate little guilt or remorse, and will unscrupulously do whatever they need to do in order to meet their self-serving desires. They are typically dishonest, calculating and selfish. ASPDs are impulsive, unpredictable and apt to break or ignore rules and laws. They are indifferent to the needs of others, especially to those with whom they are in a relationship. They often lack consideration for others and are irresponsible in most of their relationships. ASPDs frequently have chronic employment problems, as they either are fired, quit or simply walk out of their jobs when bored or annoyed. As pathological liars and cunning manipulators, ASPDs are typically unfaithful and exploitative in relationships. ASPDs often have a history of legal problems and have the capacity for belligerence, aggression and violence.

Other diagnostic terms associated with ASPD include sociopathy (sociopaths) or psychopathy (psychopaths). In 1994, with the DSM-IV, the diagnosis "sociopathy" and "sociopath" were replaced by "antisocial personality disorder." The psychological and psychiatric community deemed the change necessary because the primary diagnostic trait/symptom for sociopathy was a "violation of social norms," which was considered subjective and ever-changing. The updated diagnosis, antisocial personality disorder, required more behavior specific and concrete diagnostic criteria.

Psychopaths versus ASPD's

Before 1980, the terms "psychopathy" and "sociopathy" were used interchangeably. Although they still share behavioral similarities such as dishonesty, manipulativeness, and the lack of empathy and remorse, they are considered different diagnoses. While most psychopaths meet the criteria for ASPD, not all ASPDs are psychopaths.

Psychopaths are generally understood to be dangerous, violent and controlling individuals who lack compassion and regret. They rely on manipulation, violence and intimidation to control others and satisfy their selfish needs. They are unable to feel/experience guilt, remorse or anxiety about any of their actions. Moreover, ASPD's and psychopaths internalize and externalize their pathological behavior differently. For example, "[ASPDs] are seen as disorganized and rash, making extreme responses to normal situations. They lack impulse control. Psychopaths, by contrast, are highly organized, often secretly planning out and fantasizing about their acts in great detail before actually committing them, and sometimes manipulating people around them" (wiki.answers.com). Although psychopathy is associated with conduct problems, criminality or violence, many psychopaths are not violent. Despite having "psycho" being a root word of the diagnosis, psychopaths are rarely psychotic. For the purposes of this book, psychopathy, sociopathy and antisocial personality disorder diagnoses will be treated as one disorder – antisocial personality disorder.

The understanding of the antisocial personality disorder is inescapably connected to the history of the mental health field and the norms and social mores of the times. To illustrate, in 1812, ASPD was referred to as "moral alienation of the mind;" in 1891, "psychopathic inferiority;" in 1897, "moral imbecility;" in 1904, "morally depraved;" in 1915, "psychopathic personalities;" in 1941, "psychopath;" in 1951 (in the DSM) "sociopathic personality disturbance;" in 1968 (DSM-II), "antisocial personality, personality disorder;" and in 1980 (DSM-III), " antisocial personality disorder." Although the term "antisocial personality disorder" remained unchanged with the 1994 publication on the DSM-IV, the clinical understanding and subsequent definition of it has advanced.

According to the DSM-IV-TR, 3% of men and 1% of women in America have antisocial personality disorder. It is estimated that 50-75% of the prison population in the United States meet the criteria for antisocial personality disorder, but only 15-25% exceed the cut-off point for psychopathy (Hare, 2003 & 2008).

The DSM-IV-TR™ (2000) diagnostic criteria for antisocial personality disorder are:

- Callous unconcern for the feelings of others.

- Incapacity to experience guilt or to profit from experience, particularly punishment. Lack of remorse, as indicated by being indifferent to or rationalizing having hurt, mistreated or stolen from another.

- Gross and persistent attitude of irresponsibility, as indicated by repeated failure to sustain consistent work behavior or honor financial obligations.

- Disregard for social norms, rules and obligations.

- Failure to conform to lawful behaviors, as indicated by repeatedly performing acts that are grounds for arrest.

- Incapacity to maintain enduring relationships, though having no difficulty in establishing them.

- Very low tolerance to frustration and a low threshold for discharge of aggression, including violence.

- Reckless disregard for safety of self or others.

- Impulsiveness or failure to plan ahead.

- Markedly prone to blame others or to offer plausible rationalizations for the behavior that has brought the person into conflict with society.

- Deception, as indicated by repeatedly lying, use of aliases or conning others for personal profit or pleasure.

- Irritability and aggressiveness, as indicated by repeated physical fights or assaults.

Among all of the emotional manipulation disorders, ASPD is the most narcissistic in nature. ASPDs are almost always entitled, grandiose, egotistic, self-absorbed, selfish, and self-centered. Much like those with NPD, they have an inflated sense of self, a deep-seated sense of superiority and are egocentric and arrogant. Their sense of entitlement is off the charts as they believe that they should not be held accountable for their behavior nor should they have to follow rules or laws. One could argue the point that ASPDs are even more narcissistic than those with narcissistic personality disorder! It is important to note that, even though all ASPDs are narcissistic, not all NPDs are antisocial.

Living by the Pleasure Principle

ASPDs live their life by the "pleasure principle:" if it feels good and they are able to avoid consequences, they will do it! They live their life in the fast lane – to the extreme – seeking stimulation, excitement and pleasure from wherever they can get it. They get it while they can…because every day brings them new opportunities to feel good. Whether it is with sex, drugs, alcohol or spending, they live like there is no tomorrow. Their never-ending search for gratification may devolve into an addiction, which often exponentially increases the levels of chaos and dysfunction in their relationships. Adding an addiction disorder to ASPD is like throwing gasoline onto a fire. Therefore, it should be no surprise that ASPD is more common with alcohol and drug abusers (Lewis et al., 1983). Approximately 15-20% of male alcoholics and 10% of female alcoholics would qualify for an ASPD diagnosis, compared with 4% of men and approximately .8% of women in the US population (Cadoret et al., 1984; Anthenelli et al., 1994).

More than the other emotional manipulator disorders, ASPDs are unwilling and unable to participate mutually and reciprocally in any relationship. According to the continuum of self theory, the ASPDs CSV will always be a (+5). Their self-orientation is defined by complete self-absorption, selfishness, and disregard for the needs of others. With that said, ASPDs are able to charm others into believing they really do care about them, want to sacrifice for them, and that their generosity is heartfelt and unconditional. This of course is just a facade as they are really selfish and callously indifferent to those with whom they have feigned a caring and loving relationship.

Individuals with ASPD are unable to maintain enduring relationships and are incapable of empathy or attachment. They typically display shallow and insincere emotions. As pathological/compulsive liars and con artists, they are easily able to conceal the truth from others. They rely on deception and fraudulence to maintain their facade of likability, as well as to disarm others so that they are open to their manipulative harm. For some ASPDs, conning others is a sport; not only do they gain from their exploits, they also experience the pleasure of the hunt. ASPDs often use aliases to cover up their secrets, including multiple identities and secret lives.

Since ASPDs are incapable of empathy and emotional warmth, they rely on deceptive charm or fake likability to mask their real nature and self-serving agenda. They hide their deceiving and manipulative selves behind an affable and superficially charming exterior. They often fake or charm their way into relationships, as they are masters at pretending to be sincere, friendly and altruistic. Charm, charisma and personal magnetism are all precisely wielded to manipulate others' emotions in order to exploit and personally profit from them.

Some ASPDs have honed their superficial wit and charm into a precise skill set that, when done well, will fool almost anyone, including those who have known them their whole life. Their victims, or those who have confused their likable charm with who they really are, are often oblivious to their secretive agenda. These master "choreographers" and "actors" are so believable; they certainly could earn an Oscar. Charm is the metaphorical mask or costume that enables ASPDs to blend in with society and achieve their dishonest and sociopathic goals. When their secretive plans are uncovered, often through an accident or a mistake, their victims are mortified and shocked at their gullibility.

Ted Bundy (a psychopathic murderer) was described as handsome, charismatic, articulate and very likable. He exploited his victims by knowing exactly what to say and what they wanted to hear. Charm got him close to the people that he would eventually brutally murder. Ted Bundy was convicted of 30 homicides in seven states; the true total remains unknown. Bernie Madoff is another example of a charming, clever and highly exploitive ASPD. Madoff, a white-collar ASPD, stole $50 billion dollars from unsuspecting investors, which included friends, family, charities, senior citizens and others. He literally robbed hundreds of their life savings. Many of his victims lost their entire personal savings and some their entire retirement nest egg. Friends and family were shocked when they learned of Madoff's crimes. It was reported that virtually no one suspected that Madoff was capable of such grievous crimes. To most of Madoff's friends, family and business associates, he was known as kind, sensitive, generous and trustworthy.

An excerpt from a New York Times 2009 article best summarizes Bernie Madoff's ASPD (psychopathic) tendencies.

To some, Bernard L. Madoff was an affable, charismatic man who moved comfortably among power brokers on Wall Street and in Washington, a winning financier who had all the toys: the penthouse apartment in Manhattan, the shares in two private jets, the yacht moored off the French Riviera…There was, of course, another side to Mr. Madoff, who is 70. Reclusive, at times standoffish and aloof, this Bernie rarely rubbed elbows in Manhattan's cocktail circuit or at Palm Beach balls. This Bernie was quiet, controlled and closely attuned to his image, down to the most minute details. While he managed billions of dollars for individuals and foundations, he shunned one-on-one meetings with most of his investors, wrapping himself in an Oz-like aura, making him even more desirable to those seeking access.

So who was the real Bernie Madoff? And what could have driven him to choreograph a $50 billion Ponzi scheme, to which he is said to have confessed? An easy answer is that Mr. Madoff was a charlatan of epic proportions, a greedy manipulator so hungry to accumulate wealth that he did not care whom he hurt to get what he wanted.

(Creswell & Landon, 2009)

ASPDs are adept in faking or imitating love and commitment in a relationship. They are able to avoid detection by keeping their deeper and more central sociopathic/psychopathic tendencies meticulously hidden. They act the part of a loving and caring person, especially when it helps them obtain what they value most: sex, financial security, someone to care for them – or just the status of being in a relationship. Moreover, they are capable of using a person (a relationship with them) as a cover or "camouflage" of sorts. Through a fake "normal" relationship, they give themselves legitimacy; a perfect alibi for their secret side. The dual lives enable them to freely engage in furtive and despicable activities without detection. This is why so many people are shocked when they hear about *the sociopath next door*.[14]

Master Manipulators

ASPDs easily, and without guilt or shame, can exploit their partners for financial and/or personal gain. They are successful liars, manipulators and thieves because they are so believably the opposite. Their facade of benevolence, kindness and patience successfully covers their real "cold-hearted" nature. Their detached nature and their disregard for the feelings and welfare of others are hidden below their likable and affable exterior.

---

[14] This is also a title of a very good book on ASPDs by Martha Stout.

ASPDs justify their dishonest, manipulative and harmful actions through a distorted and bizarre set of beliefs, such as, "take what you want or someone will beat you to it," "it's a dog-eat-dog world...get what you can when you can" or "sometimes you're the bug and sometimes you're the windshield." When confronted by their victims or even by the police/court system, they

typically vehemently and believably deny any wrongdoing. They get the spotlight off of them, and typically blame the victim for their antisocial behavior because of their "stupidity" or "gullibility."

ASPDs are intolerant of anyone who tries to prevent them from getting what they want or believe they need. They can be dangerously threatening, aggressive and abusive to anyone who attempts to get in their way or prevent them from obtaining what they want. When confronted or provoked, they are easily enraged to the point of violence. ASPDs who are physically, verbally, psychologically or sexually abusive, behave in this manner because they feel entitled to do so and are unable to regulate their aggressive or violent impulses. ASPDs experience little to no empathy or guilt for the people they harm. Emotions like guilt or remorse are incomprehensible to them.

Naturally, codependents or individuals with a CSV of (-5) are susceptible to ASPDs' beguiling and manipulative charm. They are not only completely others oriented (self-orientation) they also lack the psychological abilities to discern when someone is selfishly/narcissistically manipulating them. Codependents are "ideal" partners for the abusive and domestically violent ASPDs. By nature of their others oriented psychopathology, codependents are susceptible to a domestically violent ASPD's strategy to systematically weaken, deflate and, consequently, strip them of real and perceived feelings of personal efficacy and power.

CHAPTER 14

Why We Can Reach Codependents and Not Emotional Manipulators

The manner in which a child coped with their emotional manipulator parent's narcissism is ultimately expressed in his capability to recognize and seek help for his adult problems. The child who is destined to become codependent was able to make his emotional manipulator parent feel good about their damaged narcissistic selves. As a direct result of the child's "pleasing" and "gifted" nature, the child destined to be a codependent provided their narcissistic parent with a psychological vehicle to act out their distorted fantasies of being a giver of life, a natural nurturer and an exemplary caregiver. This pleasing child understood that by providing their narcissistic parent with feelings of pride, joy, and personal comfort, they would dramatically increase the likelihood that they would be "loved" and cared for, albeit conditionally. Unlike the child who could not please or be a "gifted" child (a future emotional manipulator), this child would not be traumatized in a manner that would necessitate the defense mechanisms of disassociation and repression. Consequently, this child would develop into an adult who would have the capacity to understand his problems, recall them, and if necessary seek help for them.

Because codependents experienced less childhood trauma and did not have to repress it, their mental health is superior to that of an emotional manipulator. Compared to emotional manipulators, they are far more self-aware, introspective, self-analytical and inherently capable of accepting their problems and deficiencies. They have an ability to be conscious of their shortcomings without experiencing self-loathing and humiliating shame. Instead of projecting blame on others for their problems, codependents turn their focus inward, which might include blaming themselves and suffering in silence. They are therefore able to understand, reflect on and be honest about their negative emotional experiences. Although they do not openly share their inadequacies, they are able to accept them, consider their negative and harmful nature and, if necessary, talk about them. Unlike an emotional manipulator, they are not typically reflexively angry and defensive when given constructive feedback about their problems, mistakes and/or deficiencies. Codependents are, therefore, more apt to reach out for personal or professional help as they feel less threatened by it. They are significantly more open and amenable to the psychotherapy process.

Emotional Manipulators More Damaged than Codependents

As described in preceding chapters, emotional manipulators are significantly more psychologically impaired or damaged than are codependents. When faced with the necessity to participate in psychotherapy, they typically become resistant, guarded, and defensive. Because of their characteristic grandiosity, entitlement and propensity for denial, emotional manipulators are unable to recognize and consequently seek help for their personal or relational problems. When pushed to seek individual or relationship psychotherapy, they often adamantly refuse because they don't see a reason for it. Their rejection and disdain of psychotherapy is distinctly connected to their emotional fragility, shame-based personalities and low levels of self-esteem, all of which they are largely unaware. Simply put, their narcissism precludes them from recognizing their part in a relationship problem. Moreover, it prevents them from identifying their personal or psychological problems. Hence, emotional manipulators rarely seek psychotherapy.

Codependents have a greater array of emotional resources and psychological abilities than emotional manipulators. It is a sad irony that, even with better mental health, codependents ultimately feel inferior to their emotional manipulator partner. Although they are psychologically healthier, they are powerless to stop their severely narcissistic partner's degradation, ridicule and control of them. Because of their tendency to not want to "upset the apple cart" or "rock the boat," codependents ultimately will choose not to seek psychotherapy in order to keep their partner from feeling threatened or angry at them. They will also avoid any discussion about the need for mental health services. Even when their relationship severely deteriorates or becomes dysfunctionally unmanageable, they will second guess the need for therapy.

Codependents often fall victim to their emotional manipulator partner's rationalizations, promises, bargaining or even threats. It is not that codependents are unable to admit their problems; instead, they avoid disclosing or confronting their problems or airing their dirty laundry, because of a very real fear of abandonment and/or reprisal. Codependents may also be avoidant, manipulative or defensive about their relationship problem as to admit to them could put them in danger. The codependent avoids going against the status quo, since it could result in painful consequences, for example, retaliation or retribution. Knowing that their emotional manipulator partner is capable of hostile retribution, whether aggressive or passive-aggressive, provides them with ample reasons to suppress or deny the need for mental health services.

Codependents Make Ideal Psychotherapy Clients

Codependents make ideal psychotherapy clients since they are not inherently paranoid or distrustful of others. They are more psychologically capable of forming trusting and emotionally connective relationships with others, especially with a psychotherapist. They are able to recall, explore and analyze their deeper psychological or relationship problems without experiencing a narcissistic injury. Because codependents often feel alone and neglected in their relationships, they are naturally more inclined to seek the sanctuary and comfort of a safe, unbiased and non-rejecting mental health professional.

Another reason codependents are more amenable to the psychotherapy process is because they typically try to please those whom they consider to be in a position of authority, i.e., a psychotherapist. Their inclination to do what they are told and to comply with the expectations of others often results in a more productive psychotherapy experience. Although a potentially dysfunctional process, their tendency to please others, including their therapist, may provide incentive for them to succeed in their therapy goals or ambitions. As motivated and hardworking clients, they typically experience a series of "aha" or breakthrough moments, which ultimately paves the way for improved mental health.

When codependents are paired with a codependency specialist or a qualified and experienced generalist psychotherapist, they are capable of experiencing a life-changing psychotherapy process. Even though codependency-specific therapy is often challenging, intensive and lengthy, it has the capacity to change the codependent's life as they are inherently capable of reaching their potential, breaking free from the bonds of their limitations and achieving a sense of strength, confidence and purpose. This author knows this to be true because he has participated in such a therapy process, as well as provided it to others throughout his career.

Without the appropriate professional background and clinical support, emotional manipulator clients are typically quite difficult and emotionally taxing, even for the most experienced and qualified clinician. As shame-based and insecure individuals, emotional manipulators react negatively to a feedback process that is inherent in the psychotherapy. They rarely consider counseling or related professional services as they are mostly incapable of conceptualizing that they have mental health problems or that they could be the cause of their relationship difficulties. Instead, they reject responsibility for their problems, casting blame everywhere except on themselves.

As children, they survived their personality-disordered or addicted parent by emotionally shutting down and disassociating from the trauma they endured. As an adult, their traumatizing childhood is bottled up, permanently blocked and repressed from their awareness behind an impenetrable psychological barrier. Instead of being conscious of their harrowing past, they identify with their projected narcissistic self: superior, faultless, grandiose and entitled. Because of their inability to see their real damaged selves, and their sensitivity to perceived failures, judgments, constructive feedback and criticism, emotional manipulators are more fragile and, consequently, unwilling to participate in the psychotherapy process.

Emotional Manipulators Struggle with Psychotherapy

Emotional manipulators who partake in psychotherapy are often resistant and unwilling to accept any responsibility for their problems. They reflexively react to negative feedback as hostile and unfair judgments of themselves. When confronted with their wrong-doing, acting-out or a problem for which they are responsible, they are quick to avoid accountability. Emotional manipulators typically defend themselves by denying accusations, blaming others, manipulatively casting themselves as victims and bullying others into accepting responsibility. Denial and blame are the most typical defense strategies that emotional manipulators use in psychotherapy. Acknowledging their problems would be tantamount to admitting that there is something fundamentally wrong with them.

If given a choice, emotional manipulators will choose a psychotherapist who will not challenge their tendency to blame others and who is non-judgmental, supportive, reflective and passive in their psychotherapy approach. Humanistic, or client-centered psychotherapy is one such approach that matches the emotional manipulator's psychological capacities and personal expectations. Client-centered therapists rarely ask probing questions, make diagnoses or ascribe responsibility or blame to their clients. According to a client-centered therapy article in the *Harvard Mental Health Letter* (2006),

"The [client-centered] therapist…create(s) an atmosphere in which clients can communicate their feelings with certainty that they are being understood rather than judged."

All clients, especially emotional manipulators, experience a client-centered psychotherapist as safe, non-threatening, empathic, affirming and supportive. Although client-centered psychotherapy can most certainly make emotional manipulators feel good about themselves, it is not effective at treating the emotional manipulator's psychopathology. Moreover, the client-centered psychotherapist who is not familiar with the emotional manipulation disorders may unintentionally enable an emotionally manipulative client's narcissistic world view. By doing so, they could inadvertently put the codependent partner at risk of emotional or physical harm.

If an emotional manipulator is coerced into therapy or they take part in order to avoid a threat or a consequence, they will proceed with caution and defensiveness. Participating in an environment where they are expected to communicate, problem-solve and take responsibility would undoubtedly make them feel threatened or imperiled. To escape the spotlight of accountability, they may attempt to sabotage or derail the psychotherapy process. They may call into question the therapist's background, education, gender or therapy approach. They may also try to discredit the therapist by picking apart their personality, the way they look or disrupt the therapy process by complaining about the cost, insisting that they either cannot afford it or that it is not worth it.

When in therapy, especially marital or couples therapy, emotional manipulators often begin with an incredulous and grandiose position, insisting that they are misunderstood and not guilty of the problems attributed to them. True to their narcissistic core, they not only reject culpability for the problematic behavior or situation that necessitated therapy, they are also insulted and angered by any allegations of such wrongdoing. If the emotional manipulator's incredulous and offended reactions approach doesn't sway the therapist, which is usually the case, they will attempt to charm the therapist into believing that they are actually the victim or the aggrieved party. If this manipulative tactic does not work, they may then resort to rationalizing their conduct as either being necessary or normal. The emotional manipulator might even attribute their misbehavior to their partner, insisting that if they were treated in a specific way, the problems would not have occurred.

If the emotional manipulator still cannot manipulate the therapist or the therapy process, then he or she may become passive aggressive or overtly angry and belligerent – unleashing their narcissistic rage. If the therapist consequently sets clinically appropriate boundaries, for example, requiring this client to cease his disruptive and inappropriate expressions of anger, then it is likely that the emotional manipulator will respond with dismissive arrogance or threats to quit therapy. Typically, emotional manipulators terminate therapy when the therapist remains neutral while being consistent with boundaries for acceptable behavior.

Emotional manipulators are adept at manipulating their codependent companion, and even the psychotherapist, into believing their promises to change or stop their disruptive, harmful and dysfunctional behavior. They also may cleverly procrastinate or postpone their promise to participate in therapy long enough until their partner resumes their codependent pattern of forgiveness and forgetfulness, thereby releasing them from blame or responsibility. Similarly, emotional manipulators may also manipulatively comply with their partner's absolute insistence on therapy in order to avoid a negative consequence, e.g., divorce or breakup. They simply play the role of the willing and motivated psychotherapy client just long enough to get the heat off of themselves so the relationship can resume its "normal" dysfunctional nature.

Even with specialized training and experience, providing psychotherapy to emotional manipulators is exceptionally challenging. Unfortunately, a minority of psychotherapists are trained and experienced with personality disordered clients. It is common knowledge that a majority of psychotherapists are uncomfortable working with emotional manipulators, as they experience them as extraordinarily difficult and resistant clients. Consequently, positive psychotherapy outcomes for emotional manipulators are notoriously lower than for codependents.

Less knowledgeable and experienced therapists naturally fall prey to the emotional manipulator's beguiling nature, distorted rationalizations, excuses and victim stance. Unskilled or under-supervised therapists are ill-equipped to go up against the emotional manipulator's manipulative, evasive, intimidating and/or aggressive personality traits. These therapists may unfairly give the emotional manipulator more leeway in therapy to avoid outbursts, confrontation, or an abrupt termination. They may also unintentionally get drawn into the emotional manipulator's web of lies, deceit and manipulation. Inappropriate and uninformed psychotherapy approaches are not only harmful, but also have the potential to empower and enable the emotional manipulator while disempowering and dismissing their codependent partner. Therefore, unqualified therapists may unintentionally provide unethical and reckless psychotherapy services to their emotional manipulator clients.

If a mental health provider is afflicted with one of the emotional manipulator disorders, he or she may unintentionally enable the emotional manipulator clients' distorted and self-serving narcissistic perspective. The therapist, who is unawareness of their own psychopathology, is susceptible to collusion or triangulation with their emotional manipulator clients. Triangulation is a relationship concept that describes how conflict is played out in a three-person relationship (triad). When conflict between two individuals in a relationship escalates, one, or both, may seek an alliance with a third person in order to prove their point, gain power or hurt the other. The third person, or the triangulated individual, is often unaware that they are being manipulated. The triangulated individual, if conscious of his or her role, can wield considerable manipulative force on the relationship. More often than not, the triangulated individual, such as a personality disordered marital therapist, is not conscious of their collusion with their clients.

The treatment prognosis for emotional manipulators is poor, as the disorder(s) are deeply ingrained and resistant to treatment/psychotherapy. According to AllPsych.com, the prognosis for the three emotional manipulator personality disorders is as follows:

Narcissistic Personality Disorder:

Prognosis is limited and based mainly on the individual's ability to recognize their underlying inferiority and decreased sense of self-worth. With insight and long- term therapy, the symptoms can be reduced in both number and intensity.

Borderline Personality Disorder:

Prognosis is difficult to assess. While the disorder is chronic in nature, gradual improvements with work are definitely seen. While it is difficult for anyone to change major aspects of their personality, the symptoms of this disorder can be reduced in both number and intensity. Long term treatment is almost always required.

Antisocial Personality Disorder:

Prognosis is not very good because of two contributing factors. First, because the disorder is characterized by a failure to conform to society's norms, people with this disorder are often incarcerated because of criminal behavior. Secondly, a lack of insight into the disorder is very common. People with antisocial personality disorder typically see the world as having the problems, not him or herself, and therefore rarely seek treatment. If progress is made, it is typically over an extended period of time.

Another reason for negative therapy outcomes for emotional manipulators is that the therapist is not trained and does not receive adequate supervision for the specific mental health disorder. A therapist's reflexive adverse reaction to their clients can also result in undesirable therapy outcomes. A therapist's unconscious reaction to their client's psychopathology is known as counter-transference. To understand countertransference, it is first necessary to define both transference and countertransference. The definitions are as follows:

Transference: When a client unconsciously redirects their feelings for a significant person in their life onto another person, i.e., feelings for their mother onto their therapist. Transference is likely to occur in a psychotherapeutic relationship since the safe and unconditional nature of a therapist is unconsciously reminiscent of the fantasy parent-child relationship. A client's transference may manifest itself in a variety of ways such as idealization, attraction, dependence, rage, hatred, mistrust, and even revulsion. Clients who are emotional manipulators often exhibit destructive forms of transference, while codependents experience positive forms. In others words, codependents are more likely to idealize and depend on their therapist, whereas emotional manipulators are more likely to be angry or suspicious of them.

Countertransference: This can be a therapist's reaction to the client's transference or when a therapist directs their own personal feelings and unresolved conflicts onto their client. To illustrate, if a therapist was abused by a borderline personality disordered parent, and they have not sufficiently resolved this trauma and are not involved in ongoing clinical supervision, it is likely they may reflexively and unconsciously respond negatively to clients with the same personality traits.

Countertransference can take the shape of sharp reactivity, disapproval and/or impatience to a client. Conversely, it can also appear as an overly positive and protective reaction to their client. Whether triggered by a client's transference, or if the client's personality or behaviors reminds them of a significant individual or relationship of their past, therapists must keep a close eye on their reactions to their clients. A therapist's attunement to their own countertransference is nearly as critical as understanding their client's transference.

A list of known effective treatment options for the emotional manipulator personality disorders will follow. It should be noted that this is not a comprehensive and complete list of all known treatment options for these disorders. These treatment options utilize one or a combination of therapy approaches, i.e., individual, family, marital/couples, or group therapy.

Treatment for NPD

Psychoanalytic psychotherapy
Functional analytic psychotherapy
Self Psychology therapy
Schema-focused therapy (SFT)
Cognitive behavioral therapy(CBT)
Dialectical behavior therapy (DBT)

Treatment for BPD

Transference-Focused Psychotherapy (TFP)
Schema-focused therapy (SFT)
Dialectical behavior therapy (DBT)
Cognitive behavioral therapy(CBT)

Treatment for ASPD

Unfortunately, no research-based treatment approaches have consistently been proven to be effective for antisocial personality disorder. The following are used with only limited success:

Specialized Individual Therapy

CBT
Psychoeducation
Family support
Medication for co-occurring disorders, i.e., depression, anxiety,
Bipolar disorder, etc.
Addiction treatment/counseling
Prison (Not really a treatment approach, but it does keep society safe)

CHAPTER 15

The "Golden Rule" of the Helping Professions

It is a common belief within the mental health field that a psychotherapist's competence is often compromised when they work with clients who share the very same problem that they have, but are neither aware of nor motivated to work on. Early in my career, I came to the conclusion that in order to become a truly empathetic, competent and integrity-based psychotherapist, I would need to resolve my own propensity to be attracted to emotional manipulators. I would need to practice the very same standard of mental and emotional health as I promoted in my professional practice. My commitment to resolve my personal issues, which includes my codependent propensity, is the basis and inspiration for this chapter.

The "Golden Rule" may be one of the most universally accepted axioms in the world. The modern version, "Do unto others as you would have them do unto you," speaks to the importance of reciprocity and mutuality in relationships, as well as the need to avoid double standards. It is an ethical and moral imperative that is beautiful in its simplicity, universality and applicability. The Golden Rule has a long history dating back to 1780 BC in ancient Babylon (Bond, 1998). Five religious references to the Golden Rule include:

- The Bible/Old Testament - Leviticus 19:18: "You shall not take vengeance or bear a grudge against your kinsfolk. Love your neighbor as yourself: I am the LORD."

- Rabbi Hillel (fl. 30 BC - 10 AD): "That which is unpleasant to you, do not to your neighbor. That is the whole law and the rest but it's exposition."

- The Second Testament - Luke 6:31: "And as ye would that men should do to you, do ye also to them likewise."

- Confucius: "What you do not wish for yourself, do not do to other." (Riegel, 2012)

- Hinduism: "One should never do that to another which one regards as injurious to one's own self." Brihaspati, Mahabharata (Anusasana Parva, Section CXIII, Verse 8)

If the Golden Rule was adapted to the helping professions, I believe it would go something like this: "*Do unto yourself as you would expect others to do unto themselves.*" The "Golden Rule" of the helping professions speaks to the necessity for all helping professionals to apply the advice or direction we give to others to ourselves. It is an ethical mandate for us helping professionals to "practice what we preach."

As people who are entrusted with so much responsibility, professional helpers should conduct themselves according to a standard that prohibits them from providing services that they themselves need. Moreover, these professionals should not provide a service if their own unaddressed or untreated condition blocks their capacity to effectively help their clients. Just like the original Golden Rule, the Golden Rule of the Helping Professions emphasizes the need to avoid hypocrisy or double standards in the manner in which helping professionals provide professional services. Asking clients or patients to follow advice that the professional helper has no intention of practicing themselves, e.g., get help for alcoholism or treatment for our sexual abuse trauma puts clear and definite constraints on their capabilities and the quality of services they provide. The "Golden Rule of the Helping Professions" is indeed a moral and ethical mandate.

As people who are entrusted with so much responsibility, professional helpers should conduct themselves according to a standard that prohibits them from providing services that they themselves need. Moreover, helping professionals should not provide a service if their own unaddressed or untreated condition blocks their capacity to effectively help their clients. Just like the original Golden Rule, the Golden Rule of the Helping Professions emphasizes the need to avoid hypocrisy or double standards in the manner in which helping professionals provide professional services. Asking clients or patients to follow professional advice that the professional helper has no intention of practicing themselves, e.g., get help for alcoholism or treatment for our sexual abuse trauma puts clear and definite constraints on their capabilities and the quality of services they provide. The "Golden Rule of the Helping Professions" is indeed a moral and ethical mandate.

This author ascribes to the conventional belief that all therapists should periodically participate in their own therapy throughout their careers.

A blog entitled, "Therapist, Heal Thyself," speaks to the importance of self-care for psychotherapists.

"I need to be able to sort out my own personal issues from those of my patient and that is very difficult without having done work in therapy. Just as I cannot see my own back without a mirror, so too I cannot see my shadow and blind spots without benefit of the mirror of therapy. It is not a function of how happy one's childhood was because none of us come to adulthood without issues, without shadow. It is matter of the major importance of self-education, the kind that can only come, I believe, through the process of engaging in self-exploration with a good therapist."

(Cheryl Fuller, www.jung-at-heart.com, 2007)

I believe that the Golden Rule for the Helping Professions is the cornerstone of competency for all helping professionals, especially psychotherapists. Having familiarity with the client/patient's experience or knowing what it's like to be "on the other side of the couch" or "the other side of the stethoscope" creates higher levels of empathy and consequently higher levels of professionalism. It is particularly helpful in developing higher degrees of compassion, understanding and empathy for the clients/patients we serve, while also increasing our awareness and understanding of their feelings of vulnerability, anxiety or fear. The Golden Rule for the Helping Professions brings us to "talking the talk while walking the walk" or as Benjamin Franklin once said, "Well done is better than well said."

The genesis of the idea for the Golden Rule of the Helping Professions can be traced back to my first week of graduate school at Boston University in the fall of 1987. During our orientation, our lead professor, James Day, Ph.D., asked the group of nervous graduate school newbies to raise their hands if we had ever been in psychotherapy. Naturally, of course, my hand shot up! While proudly displaying my openness to psychotherapy, I looked around and was surprised that only about twenty percent of my classmates had similarly participated in psychotherapy. Dr. Day was also surprised. I will never forget what he said: "How can you expect to enter into a career field in which you are entrusted to affect and change someone else's life, if you have not, yourself, experienced the process?" He continued with, "I promise you, by the time this program is over, you will need therapy...and if you still don't think you do, it doesn't matter, it's a requirement!" He was right; we all needed some extra help that year!

It is my belief that for us helpers to be effective, responsive and impactful to our own clients, we should seek to recognize and confront our own emotional and psychological limitations. According to Carl

Goldberg, author of *On Being a Psychotherapist* (1991): "The journey in the quest for healing and problem resolution can only happen when both the therapist and the clients share the same willingness for increased awareness and understanding of their own identity."

Based on anecdotal evidence and this author's two-and-a half decades of professional experience, it seems that a significant proportion of professional helpers had a parent who was narcissistic or an emotional manipulator. More specifically, it seems that many helping professionals are involved in personal and romantic relationships in which they are caretakers or codependents to a narcissistic partner. It is the presumption of this author that when we professional helpers were children, we learned to cope with our narcissistic parent by developing a pleasing, helpful and accommodating persona. Having developed a high tolerance for frustration, endless patience, effective listening and problem- solving skills while learning to squelch our own feelings, helped us not only survive our childhoods but also created a foundation for adult codependency. It is well known that psychotherapists (professional helpers) were cast at a young age into the role of helper or nurturer in their families. It is then logical to presume that professional helpers, especially psychotherapists, are drawn to a career that matches their unique world view, personality and psychological needs (Roe, 1964).

Given that many professional helpers did not have ideal childhoods (psychologically healthy families), psychotherapy is highly recommended, if not required. Taking the time to sort out the impact of one's childhood experiences, especially if they were traumatic, is an essential component of professional and emotional development. Professional helpers are no different from the clients they provide services to, as both share a need for emotional health as well as personal and relational stability. Professional helpers who seek services for their own psychological/personal issues increase the potential for positive outcomes with their clients. It is commonly accepted by most psychotherapists, that first-hand experience with the psychotherapy process not only may solve the therapist's problem or issue, but also creates deeper levels of empathy and compassion for their own clients.

Therapists seeking their own type of services, especially psychotherapy, is neither new nor unusual. According to 20 years of research, 84% of all psychotherapists have reportedly sought psychotherapy (Norcross & Evans, 2009). The propensity to be on both sides of the couch can be traced back to Sigmund Freud, who wrote, "Every analyst ought periodically...to enter analysis once more, at intervals of, say, five years, and without any feeling of shame in doing so" (Freud, 1937/1963, pp. 267-

268). After all, our professional qualities of empathy, patience, calmness and compassion are closely tied to our current mental health.

Because codependency is a common problem among mental health and healthcare professionals, it is critical that these professionals seek psychotherapy services early in their career. "Ideally, this should occur at the student level, because the insight that is gained will enable potential caregivers to recognize both the positive and negative aspects of their codependent behaviors and the effect that these may have on their personal and professional interactions" (Clark & Stoffel, 1992, p. 823). Therefore, it becomes incumbent upon all those in the helping professions, who were most likely children of emotional manipulators, to pursue their own journey of personal and emotional healing. Without practicing what we preach, we would be negligent and careless in our duties.

What follows expands on the Golden Rule for the Helping Professions:

- If you share the same problem as your client, your abilities and effectiveness may be compromised.

- Our mental health and our professional capabilities are intertwined.

- Our personal growth will almost always advance our professional capabilities.

- Like an oil change, every mental health and most helping professionals should seek psychotherapy at specific and necessary intervals.

- "Practice what you preach." Promoting physical and mental health in others requires you to follow your own advice or direction.

- Be a role model to your patients/clients; let them know you take care of yourself.

- We must examine our own reactions and judgments, as they are likely to represent what we do and do not like about ourselves.

- Intuitive abilities come from an unconscious experience of positive mental health.

- Your job may make you feel good, but it won't sustain you emotionally.

- Leave your work at the office.

- Learn to play and have fun when you are not working. You have a difficult job and life is short.

The Golden Rule of the Helping Professions should, therefore, remind all professional helpers and healers to do for themselves what they expect their clients to do with them. Practicing what you preach makes all the difference in establishing a remarkable career.

Conclusion

It's Never Too Late To Be Who You Might Have Been

We all come into this imperfect world, in imperfect families, as imperfect versions of ourselves. Not one of us is without a story or two about family dysfunction, economic hardships, medical limitations, self-esteem challenges and more. Through conscious choices, personal commitment, and hard work, we all can experience the world as fully competent, secure, loving and loved individuals. With a fervent belief in ourselves and a commitment to becoming the very best version of ourselves, we can achieve our God-given right to experience joy and healthy love. Taking good care of yourself, healing your emotional wounds, and unconditionally loving yourself, will bring you closer to your dreams. My very favorite quote by George Eliot exemplifies the malleable and indomitable nature of the human psyche/human spirit: "It's never too late to be who you might have been."

As a survivor of some rather challenging relationships with emotional manipulators, I must say to the codependent readers there is most definitely hope for healthy love! I am living proof that if you make a commitment to a healing and transformational process, it is possible to squelch, if not completely stop, the dysfunctional voices that our emotional manipulator parents instilled in our minds. We all have the power to terminate the commanding unconscious force that compels us to replicate our childhood trauma through our choices of dysfunctional adult romantic partners. With the help of loved ones and qualified professional services, it is possible to heal those childhood wounds that have unconsciously directed you to "dance" with the same dysfunctional partner over and over again.

I challenge the readers of this book to courageously commit to never giving up on yourselves – to never again feel powerless in a relationship that is harmful to you. The choice to change, to release yourself from the shackles of your dysfunctional past and to stop your magnetic propensity to fall in love with an emotional manipulator might be the biggest and most important change that you will ever make in your life. Stopping your own personal insanity will take perseverance and courage. It will require dedication, diligence, endurance, patience and, probably, a stint or two of psychotherapy.

I am sharing the following poem because, a long time ago, during a low point in my life, it inspired me to continue my own personal therapeutic work. It spoke to that part of my heart that yearned for true love, but was trapped by mysterious formidable and unconscious forces. David Whyte's poem, *The True Love*, encouraged me to stay true to my pledge to heal and to never lose hope for "true love." His poem was the beacon of light that, in my personal darkness, kept me focused on my pursuit of love for myself and, ultimately, for a lover who would share the wondrous experience of true and healthy love with me.

The True Love
David Whyte

There's a faith in loving fiercely the one who is rightfully yours
especially if you have waited years and especially if part of you never
believed you could deserve this loved and beckoning hand held
out to you this way.

I am thinking of faith now and the testaments of loneliness
and what we feel we are worthy of in this world.
Years ago in the Hebrides I remember an old man
who would walk every morning on the gray stones
to the shore of baying seals, who would press his
hat to his chest in the blustering salt wind and say his
prayer to the turbulent Jesus hidden in the waters.

And I think of the story of the storm and the people
waking and seeing the distant, yet familiar figure,
far across the water calling to them.
And how we are all preparing for that abrupt waking
and that calling and that moment when we have to say yes!
Except it will not come so grandly, so biblically,
but more subtly, and intimately in the face
of the one you know you have to love.
So that when we finally step out of the boat
toward them we find, everything holds us,
and everything confirms our courage.

And if you wanted to drown, you could,
but you don't, because finally, after all
this struggle and all these years,
you don't want to anymore.
You've simply had enough of drowning
and you want to live, and you want to love.
And you'll walk across any territory,
and any darkness, however fluid,
and however dangerous to take the one
hand and the one life, you know belongs in yours.

David Whyte from "The House of Belonging" and "River Flow" (1996)
Permission to reprint given by David Whyte & Many Rivers Company

Along the way, you are likely to make a mistake or two. Do not let the pain of these mistakes throw you off course. More importantly, don't second guess your commitment to yourself. There will be a payoff – I promise! In time, you will realize that you are now healthy, confident and strong enough to choose a romantic partner who is, first and foremost, a friend, and who loves, cares and respects you for who you are, not just what you can do for him or her. You also will find that your improved "relationship picker" will help you get to the point in which you are ready "to take the one hand and the one life, you know belongs in yours" (Whyte, 1996). Your improved psychological health will change the "polarity" of your human magnet. You will start to naturally repel narcissists while finding yourself irresistibly attracted to a person with whom you share deep feelings of love, respect and caring. Better yet, a person who wants to love, respect, and care for you will be attracted to you!

Go to the mirror now, and look yourself in the eye. There is a child inside of you, the child you used to be. He or she is you – a frightened child who is frozen in time because of harm suffered and endured at a young age. You know you desperately want to be released from the shackles of self-doubt, self-loathing and fear. You, and only you, can make the determination to walk down a new path in life that will certainly bring you to happiness, serenity and improved self-esteem. The decision is yours: Live with limited risk but perpetual relational dysfunction, or risk everything and choose to begin the personal/emotional work that will bring you to healthy and satisfying mutual love – true love. Make the right choice.

Emotional Manipulators and Me – The Evolution of the Concepts

The journey to understanding my own instinctual, but broken, relationship guide began well before I became a psychotherapist. I can clearly remember when, because of my out of control drug abuse, I was at the brink of self-destruction. Beginning at age 14, I had been self-medicating my emotional problems by taking copious amounts of drugs. My journey of understanding, healing and transformation began precisely in August of 1978 when, at age 17, I was hospitalized for drug abuse. Although I didn't know it at the time, I was a very sad, lonely and angry teenager.

Because my parents feared that my drug abuse would cost me my life, they sought intensive inpatient treatment for me at Riveredge Hospital in Forest Park, Illinois. I will never forget the day when I was deceived into believing that if I went to see a counselor for just one session, my parents would allow me to go to the REO Speedwagon concert with my friends. I had plans to get "wasted" before, during and after the concert. Little did I know, instead of seeing REO Speedwagon I was admitted into a mental health facility. The "one hour" counseling session turned into 90 days.

For my first two to three weeks at Riveredge, I refused to consider that my drug use had anything to do with anything other than just wanting to have fun and feel good. At the time, I was unable to face the sad truth about my life – that as far back as I could remember I had been lonely, insecure and frequently ridiculed and rejected by my peers. The drugs that I had been abusing effectively numbed my psychological pain. It took some time to break down my defenses, but after a month, I began to openly consider my sad personal reality. Feeling safe and supported by my new friends and by the hospital's counseling staff, I started to consider that my recreational use of large quantities of drugs was not really about having fun but instead, to escape, disconnect and numb my painful feelings of being unimportant and unlovable.

In about the fourth week of my treatment, following a slew of confrontational individual and group therapy sessions, I experienced a startling emotional breakthrough. In that moment, I wasn't so sure anymore how I felt about anything, including the reasons behind my drug abuse. Feeling numb and confused, I went back to my room where I felt compelled to write my very first poem. It was a very sad poem about a sad lonely person – me. It was entitled Loneliness. Writing it unleashed a torrent of emotional anguish, which was a surprise to me. Apparently, I had neatly suppressed and covered up these feelings. The act of writing it seemed to release a reservoir of long-suppressed feelings, which resulted in a crying spell that was like no other that I had previously experienced. In a flood of painful memories and realizations, for the first time in my life, I faced the sad emotional realities of my life. This poem, which is below, helped me realize how lonely and insecure I felt, while also helping me connect to my life-long feelings of being unimportant and unlovable, which I would find out later were connected to my emotionally-deprived childhood.

Loneliness
Loneliness is a feeling, which is so hard to accept.
It will gnaw at you for a lifetime.
No matter how hard you try to forget.
The pain it causes is unbearable.
Only if you knew of this pain and how it hurts.
You hope someone will understand,
But no one does.

All I ask for is one mere favor.
Just a friend, someone who cares, someone who loves,
Someone who will give me strength.
And how I need this.
Many times my dreams are shattered.
But I swear, it is ever fulfilled,
You will see me with an outstretched hand.

I am ready now to experience something I have craved for so long.
If it takes a fight to get over this dreadful feeling,
I am ready,
I am waiting.

Just let me get knocked down,
You will see me get right back up.
And yet I will still fight.
Fierce and determined I will have to be.

You might even see me bruised and injured.
But I will never give up.

Here I am.
Just maybe, Just maybe if I shed enough tears,
I might look and notice,
Just maybe there will be someone at my side.
Someone who really cares,
Someone who understands.

How excited I get at this thought.
A dream it may sound to be,
But if it is, I beg of you,
Please do not wake me up!

Ross Rosenberg (age 17)

With this breakthrough, I was free to openly sift through the emotionally fractured nature of my life. With the help of the very talented treatment staff, I began to piece together the reasons behind my self-destructive drug abuse. I had learned that no amount of drugs would ever be able to take away my deeper emotional insecurities. I become aware that, as far back as I could remember (back to age five), I had been a lonely child who was emotionally overlooked by his parents. At the hospital I began to piece together my tendency to deny, rationalize, and misplace my sadness and anger toward my parents, who seemed to have ignored my emotional needs. Perhaps the biggest breakthrough of my treatment was when I fully experienced my anger and resentment toward my parents, especially my father, who was unable to nurture their sensitive and emotional first-born son.

With the help of the hospital staff, I was able to understand and eventually accept that I carried around a great deal of sadness and anger, which was a direct result of my parents' emotional absence and inability to make me feel important, worthwhile and loved. I learned that the anger and resentment I harbored toward my parents for not being emotionally present for me, both as a child and an adolescent, had a disturbing effect on my psychological health. It became abundantly clear that I relied on drugs to transport me from my feelings of anger, insecurity, disconnection and invisibility. I learned that escaping through drug abuse would never truly alter my emotional reality; at best, it just covered it up.

The treatment I received at Riveredge most notably helped me connect my drug abuse problems to my troubled relationship with my parents. Although my parents provided well for many of their children's needs, especially for their physical needs, they were unable to emotionally and personally connect to their children. Neither my codependent mother nor my narcissistic father could provide me with the emotional comfort, validation and affirmation that I so desperately needed. Sadly, they were unable to comprehend that their emotionally disconnected parenting style was harmful to their children, especially me. Having parents who seemed disinterested and unmotivated to understand my emotional problems had fueled my lifelong feelings of loneliness, insecurity and anxiety about being rejected. My parents simply had no clue about my empty, sad and insecure emotional world.

As much as I have pointed out my parents' limitations, I am forever indebted to them for getting me help; it undoubtedly saved my life. It also had a profoundly positive impact on our relationship. Because of them, I was able to take the very important first step towards facing my emotional demons and seeking a path of healing and positive mental health. The Riveredge treatment staff helped transform me into a courageous young man who desired to change the course of his life – to seek better emotional and personal possibilities. They helped me to discover that I was actually talented at something – the first realization of that kind. Helping me recognize and appreciate my natural listening, empathy and problem-solving abilities steered me in the direction of a psychotherapy career. It was the first time in my life that I actually was told and believed that I had intrinsic value and could make a difference in the world in which I lived. It was October of 1978 and I was certain that I was to become a psychotherapist. I was hell bent to blaze a path toward obtaining it.

When I left the treatment facility, it felt like I had a new lease on life. I had come to accept that my parents would not be able to affirm, appreciate and value me in the manner that I needed. My Riveredge experience helped me understand that a healthy relationship with my parents would require me to become independent from them, while also maintaining a loving and connected relationship. I knew if I went to college as planned for me, I would still be tied into my Dad's conditions, which would only re-trigger my anger and resentment toward him. I no longer wanted to jump through anyone's hoops to get validation or affirmation. It was time for me to break free from the dysfunctional grip that my family had on me.

I took a leap of faith and, with a mix of excitement and courage, I made a life-changing decision to join the military. Enlisting in the army during peacetime, being stationed in Japan, and having a coveted military intelligence job with top secret security clearance enticed me to make a four-year life-changing commitment. The choice put me on an exciting, but frightening, road to personal, emotional and financial independence. The irony of my decision has never been lost on me: I left the controlling self-centeredness of my father for the controlling self-centeredness of the military; go figure. All in all, it was one of my best life decisions. It was my earliest experience of feeling pride in myself while also experiencing significance, validation and appreciation from my parents. For the first time in my life, we were relating to each other respectfully and lovingly (with some natural limitations).

My military experiences helped me to mature, further my confidence in myself and, most importantly, fuel my desire to become a psychotherapist. It was a very rewarding four year period in my life. Not only had I traveled the world, made great friends and matured, I was able to make major inroads at healing and reconciling my relationship with my parents. After my four year military obligation, I was ready to go to college and pursue my goal to become a psychotherapist. Thanks to veterans' benefits, a small savings account and financial aid, I was able to pursue a major in psychology at Towson State University, in Towson, Maryland without depending on my parent's seemingly conditional help. After four years in college, which included further growth of my relationship with my parents, I pursued a master's degree from Boston University.

One of the most influential moments of my college/graduate school life occurred in 1988, while taking the graduate school course, Family Systems Theories. The entire grade for the course would be based solely based on one term paper that had to be entitled, "How I Differentiated from my Family of Origin." The only instruction was to write a research-based paper using two family systems theories to explain how we learned to differentiate, or emotionally separate, from our own families. It was a perfectly timed academic and personal challenge as I had already started my "research" on it when I was a teenager at Riveredge Hospital. Little did I know that this paper would set in motion a more complete and profound awareness of my family's influence on me emotionally, personally and relationally, despite the 800 miles that separated us.

This graduate level paper helped me to tie together the multiple influences that had shaped me psychologically. This monumental writing assignment helped me comprehend how my lonely and insecure childhood was connected to the challenges and problems I experienced in my adult relationships. Although I garnered a tremendous amount of insightful and illuminating psychological information about my family, and consequently myself, I was not yet prepared to process all of it. Like a good bottle of wine, time was needed to help my own maturation process. Although I did not know it at the time, the full value of the graduate course assignment would be evident 10 years after I graduated from Boston University. It is maddening to realize that, in 1988, I may have had all the answers about how to achieve stable and mutually satisfying intimate relationships. But, as with most people who are in the process of personal transformation, time, patience, and good psychotherapy are needed.

My psychotherapy career began in 1988 at age 27, four months after I graduated from Boston University. With diploma in hand and stoked with enthusiasm and excitement for my long-awaited psychotherapy career, I quickly found employment. I was hired to provide counseling and addiction-related services in a rural counseling center in central Iowa – a far cry from Boston! It took no time at all for me to adapt to my new profession, which I absolutely loved! I quickly developed a passion for working with adults who were survivors of childhood abuse or neglect as well as clients who struggled with habitual dysfunctional relationships.

Like many therapists right out of graduate school, my training was characterized by the old adage "baptism by fire." Although I left graduate school with a head full of pertinent psychological and psychotherapeutic information, it wasn't until I actually started doing the job that I learned the "how-tos" of the profession. It quickly became evident that the more I was aware of my own dysfunctional relationship patterns, especially my codependency, the more I was able to facilitate growth and healing with my codependent clientele. The connection between my own and my client's mental health had never been more evident. Before I knew it, I was impacting the lives of my clients. This was extraordinarily satisfying considering I was so new on the psychotherapy scene! Achieving my 17-year-old dream of becoming a psychotherapist who was going to help others with their problems, just like therapist had helped me, was of a great moment of triumph for me!

Early on in my career I developed an interest in codependency – as it resonated with my own personal and relational struggles. In familiar territory, I felt equipped and capable of helping my codependent clients with their dysfunctional and self-defeating personal and relationship problems. Thanks to my previous personal work on my own family-related issues, I was quick to recognize the connection between my clients' history of child abuse, trauma and/or neglect and their dysfunctional adult relationship patterns. I took notice that my codependent clients seemed almost always to come from dysfunctional families in which one parent was a codependent and the other a narcissist or an addict. By realizing this connection, I was better equipped to guide my clients toward a better understanding of their predilection for dysfunctional relationship choices.

My positive and fruitful psychotherapy experiences, both as an adolescent and as an adult, had also helped me connect the importance of personal growth with my counseling abilities. Not only have I never been shy about seeking psychotherapy, I find it personally rewarding and enjoyable. I was like a sponge, wanting to soak up as much personal insight as possible. Psychotherapy wasn't always a "cakewalk," as there were some very difficult times in my adult life for which psychotherapy was absolutely needed. Being on "both sides of the couch" had a positive, two-fold effect on me. It helped me personally, while also demonstrating the power of the healing and transformative process to me professionally. My psychotherapy experiences have had a priceless effect on my personal and professional life.

The ideas and concepts in this book have been significantly influenced by my own personal transformation which included, but was not limited to, my own psychotherapeutic work. Over my life, psychotherapy has helped me to cope with difficult life challenges as well as tough emotional times. More importantly, it was instrumental in helping me overcome, and eventually solve, my own deeply rooted problems, which were largely connected to my childhood experience with my parents. With the help of therapy, I had come to understand that I had been a victim to my own unconscious mind, which repeatedly compelled me to reenact my childhood experience through my choice of dysfunctional romantic partners.

Perhaps my most significant and influential stint of psychotherapy was in early 1996, when I decided to end a two and half year marriage with a person who I felt was harmful and abusive. Because of my decision, what was already bitter and hostile morphed into something worse. I desperately needed help to cope with the stress of a divorce, the acrimonious actions and reactions of my wife, as well as the complicated issues surrounding my two and half year old son of whom I wanted custody. I was not prepared to cope with the conflict and the emotional pain of this divorce.

Thanks to the help I received in therapy, I was able to survive the melee of this divorce. I learned how to manage the stress and conflict of the pre- and post-divorce relationship with my son's mother, with whom I eventually would share joint custody. In therapy, I started the process of understanding my habitual attraction to women who hurt me while claiming they loved me. In the beginning, I had no explanation for why a giving, patient, and sacrificing person, such as I was, would be drawn to, and remain with women who were harmful, manipulative and abusive. By end of my therapy experience, I began to understand that I was a complicit partner in a dysfunctional relationship dance that always included me, the codependent, and a partner, who was an emotional manipulator or a narcissist.

Even with the insights gained through from my 1996 therapy sessions, I would still find myself in other dysfunctional relationships. As they say in Alcoholics Anonymous, I had not yet "hit bottom." In 1998, I fell in love with a woman who, at the time I believed with every fiber of my being, was my soul mate. When we met, we shared a seemingly perfect love at first sight experience. Not only was the physical chemistry off the charts, it felt like we had known each other our whole lives. While we reveled in the euphoric joy of our new relationship, we had not thought to consider the red flags to which we were so conveniently oblivious. We were unable to realize that we both carried a full carload of personal baggage. Since we both believed our new-found our love was perfect and that we were destined to be together for eternity, we hurried ourselves to the altar; we married six months after meeting each other.

As with my first wife, the sensation of love at first sight, was merely a mirage, created by living in a desert of solitude, loneliness and unhappiness. Shortly after our wedding, similar to my first nuptials, there was an abrupt and distinct change in our relationship. The euphoria that compelled us to tie the knot ever so quickly seemed to clear up, much like the sun acts upon early morning fog. Within six months of our marriage, unknown elements of her personality emerged. If these traits had been apparent to me prior to the wedding, I would never have consented to the union. Once again, I learned the very painful lesson that love is indeed blind…perhaps deaf, too.

By the second year of this marriage, I was, once again, in the role of care-taker, helper and sacrificial "good guy" who was not receiving any of the same positive good will in return. Marriage and my own individual therapy would not be enough to solve our relationship problems. After three years of loneliness and resentment, I decided to permanently separate from this harmful and toxic marriage. This divorce was emotionally devastating and humiliating for me, as it was my second failure in the grand institution of marriage, in which I so desperately wanted to believe. I was very angry at myself, as it felt that all the therapy work I had previously accomplished was all for naught. As a psychotherapist trying to help others in their pursuit of healthy relationships, I felt like I was an imposter. Nonetheless, the second divorce put me into an emotional tailspin that lasted 5 years – until 2006. Although it took a while, I would eventually stumble out of the fog resolved to figure out why a man, who had learned key lessons about himself and his childhood, would repeatedly make the same relationship mistakes. Clearly, I had more to learn.

A major turning point in my life occurred in April 2006, when I participated in a retreat sponsored by a men's organization called "Victories." [15] Victories, which was formerly named "Victories of the Heart," is a nonprofit organization, formed in 1985, committed to

[15] www.victoriesformen.org

helping men develop a deeper self-understanding and more honest and emotionally connective relationships. The retreat, which is referred to as "The BreakThrough Weekend" rocked my life! It helped me dig way down into the emotional infrastructure of my psychological self. On that fateful April BreakThrough Weekend, I learned that I still needed to work through my childhood anger at being neglected by my parents.

Through the ongoing personal growth groups, and other supportive and therapeutic activities, or as Victories prefers to call it, "the heart work," I have been able to powerfully connect to the origins of my codependency – my family of origin issues. My personal work with Victories has invaluably helped me to better understand the insidious nature of my dysfunctional past, and its control over my relationship choices. It facilitated (and continues to do so) a deeper comprehension of how my dysfunctional relationship patterns were distinctly connected to my unmet emotional needs as a child.

No other quote captures what I learned through my Victories experiences better than one from Anais Nin (1903-1977):

> **There came a time when the risk to remain tight in the bud**
> **was more painful than the risk it took to blossom.**

My participation in Victories nicely complemented my ongoing psychotherapeutic work. As a direct result of my participation with the Victories organization, I significantly accelerated my progress in my journey to unravel the mysteries of my dysfunctional relationship pattern. Thanks to the organization and the men in my Personal Growth Group, I was able to step out of my comfort zone and to take the risk to "blossom." I would be ready to try one more time to get it right…to find a healthy and mutually loving and caring partner. It is no coincidence that shortly after the BreakThrough Weekend; I met the love of my life, Korrel Crawford, the woman I would marry.

My journey to free myself from the unfortunate circumstances surrounding my childhood was starting to bear fruit. Most of my personal and some of my family relationships began to take on a new and improved quality. A fortunate "side effect" of my growth was the further development and refinement of my psychotherapy skills. The more I learned about myself, healed old wounds and avoided dysfunctional relationships, the more focused and effective my psychotherapy skills became. My personal and psychological gains clearly translated into more effective psychotherapy services to clients who habitually participated in dysfunctional romantic relationships. It was as if I developed an antenna of sorts that was finely tuned into the codependent-emotional manipulator experience.

As an amateur poet and a therapist who employed the use of therapeutic analogies and metaphors, I found myself referring to the codependent/narcissist relationship as a "dysfunctional dance." The more I used the dance analogy with my codependent clientele, the more they embraced it. The dance metaphor resonated with these clients, as it helped them to make sense of their reflexive and repetitive dysfunctional relationship patterns. My codependent clients especially appreciated the metaphor (and the resulting therapeutic discussions) because it helped them better understand their own codependency issues. Over time "the dysfunctional dance" became one of my standard therapeutic phrases that I used with clients who sought to free themselves from their dysfunctional relationship patterns.

As with many of my other creative techniques, this metaphor would percolate in my subconscious for a while. In 2007, I wrote an essay titled, "Codependency: Don't Dance!" Once written, my codependent clients almost unanimously praised it. The essay seemed to make intuitive sense to them as it helped them to better understand their habitual relationship patterns with their harmful romantic partners. It also served as a catalyst to many of them, because it facilitated their understandings of the powerlessness over their attraction to narcissistic partners. It became the most requested essay/article that I had ever written. Moreover, it served as the inspiration for a seminar I would eventually create: Emotional Manipulators and Codependents: Understanding the Attraction.

There has been a linear nature to the development of my understanding of codependency, narcissism and dysfunctional relationships. As the dance essay picked up steam and attracted the attention of a great many clients and therapists, it motivated me to further develop my concept of dysfunctional attraction. It also prompted me to try to gauge the magnitude of the codependent/narcissist attraction force. Eventually, I developed a psychological construct that helped identify the attraction force that compelled opposite personalities to come together into a romantic relationship. Thus was born the continuum of self theory. The continuum of self theory was streamlined, simple and even gave a mathematical explanation for the attraction dynamics observed in all relationships. It focused on the natural attraction of two opposite personality types. It became a helpful and necessary tool in furthering my clients' understanding of the unconscious mutual attraction dynamic, as explained in the dance essay. I knew I was onto something important; an explanatory concept that would be able to contribute to the understanding of human relationships.

In 2010, I created a training seminar based on the dance concept and the continuum of self idea. While writing the training, I developed yet another metaphor to explain the habitual and irresistible nature of dysfunctional attraction dynamics. I began to use a magnet and its magnetic properties to illustrate the natural and irresistible attraction of two polar opposite personality types. The "human magnet" explanation resonated with my codependent clients. It facilitated a deeper understanding of their seemingly automatic attraction to individuals with an opposite personality type who almost were always narcissistic. It also helped them make sense of why they remained with this individual despite feeling unhappy, resentful, and unappreciated.

While writing this book, I expanded the magnet metaphor into a broader explanatory concept which I named the "Human Magnet Syndrome" (chapter 7). Thanks to Jan Gomien, owner of AATP, an Illinois-based professional seminar company, I was given an opportunity to present my newest training that I titled, "The Continuum of Self: Understanding the Attraction between Narcissists & Codependents." AATP is a not-for-profit training academy established to provide professional continuing education to mental health and addiction practitioners. I was pleased with the overwhelming positive feedback I received from the seminar audience.

Such was my surprise when, in July 2011, Marnie Sullivan, a business manager for CMI/PESI (Premier Education Solutions), asked me to create a seminar based upon the "continuum of self" training. To my good fortune, it was an opportunity for me to offer the seminar to a national audience. With Marnie's encouragement, I expanded the codependent/narcissist attraction dynamic to a codependent/emotional manipulator dynamic. It was a natural extension of my hypotheses, as all the emotional manipulator disorders shared a distinct narcissistic process. [16] The new training was entitled: Emotional Manipulators and Codependents: Understanding the Attraction. To my delight, the trainings became a well-attended seminar.

Almost immediately the seminar and eventually the DVD of the seminar became a big hit. Within six months of launching the CMI/PESI seminar schedule, it became abundantly obvious that this topic area had a universal appeal. Not only was the seminar an educational experience, but it became apparent that it also had a profound emotional effect on the seminar audience. Because the topic seemed to ring true for most of the seminar participants, combined with the overwhelming support I received from friends and colleagues, I instinctively knew I had to move forward with this idea. To my great happiness, in April of 2011, CMI/PESI encouraged me to write a book based on the seminar, which they would publish.

---

[16] As explained earlier in the book, an emotional manipulator is one of three personality disorders: narcissistic, borderline or antisocial personality disorder or a person afflicted with an addiction.

Looking back, it is now clear to me that I needed to hit my own personal "bottom" before I would be motivated to figure out a way out of my seemingly instinctive and automatic tendency to perpetually sabotage myself by my choice of narcissistic romantic partners. I believe that when our personal pain becomes unbearable, or when we can no longer tolerate our unintentional but quite consequential mistakes, we are left with two choices: To continue the merry-go-round of perpetual dysfunction, or to climb, claw or wrestle ourselves out of our own dysfunctional muck. It seems to me that a power greater than ourselves (for me – God) brings us disaster or heartbreak to open our eyes and see ourselves more clearly.

Although the pain of our mistakes may motivate us to fight for sanity, we aren't shielded from the arduous and painful process of personality change. If we decide to take this psychologically healing journey, the trip will be tough for sure. We will undoubtedly experience the powerful and unmitigated forces that compel our dysfunctional relationship patterns to persist. But, when we really want to love someone who celebrates and cherishes us, we will muster the courage to walk through the fire of this emotionally daunting process. From it, we will come to understand that our mistakes will paradoxically transform into golden nuggets as wisdom. As my friend, Melody Beattie, best-selling author of Codependent No More (1986), recently explained to me, "We draw to us the experiences we need to learn." How right she is!

According to one of my favorite authors and philosophers, Paul Coelho, "When you want something, all the universe conspires in helping you to achieve it." (Coelho, 2006). Indeed, the universe heard me! Although difficult and quite challenging, I chose the path of healing. My enthusiasm to grow, learn from my mistakes and heal old wounds led me down the winding and somewhat convoluted path that culminated in writing this book. My commitment to a transformative healing process cannot be separated from my ambition to be an effective psychotherapist – one who could make a difference in the lives of others, much like those therapists who were there for me in 1978. I am exceptionally honored to be in a career field that allows me to use my own life lessons to help others who wish to break free of the dysfunctional bonds of their past. By no stretch of the imagination did all of this happen by accident. I am sure, like so many of my choices, both personal and professional, that my unconscious mind has been working on it for quite some time!

Akhtar, S. (2009). Comprehensive dictionary of psychoanalysis. London, UK: Karnac Books.

American Psychiatric Association (2000). Diagnostic and statistical manual of mental disorders dsm-iv-tr fourth edition (text review).Washington, DC: Author.

Anthenelli, R.M., Smith, T.L., Irwin, M.R., & Schuckit, M.A. (1994). A comparative study of criteria for subgrouping alcoholics: The primary/secondary diagnostic scheme versus variations of the type 1/type 2 criteria. *American Journal of Psychiatry, 151(10)*, 1468-1474.

Beattie, M. (1986). *Codependent no more: How to stop controlling others and start caring for yourself* (2nd ed.). Center City, Minnnesota:Hazelden.

Belden, R. (1990). *Iron man family outing: poems about transition into a more conscious manhood.* Rick Belden.

Boeree, C. (2006). *Personality theories: Erik Erikson 1902-1994.* Retrieved from http://webspace.ship.edu/cgboer/erikson.html

Borst, B. (2013). *Love songs: Number one songs with love in their title.* Retrieved from http://www.bobborst.com/popculture/love-songs

Bowen, M. (1993). *Family therapy in clinical practice.* Northvale, NJ: Jason Aronson, Inc.

Bowlby, J. (1969, 1983). Attachment: Attachment and Loss Volume One (1-2 ed.). New York, NY: Basic Books.

Brown, B. (Speaker). (2010). *Brené Brown: The power of vulnerability* [Lecture]. Houston, TX: Ted Conferences, LLC.

Cadoret, R.J., Troughton, E., & Widmer, R. (1984). Clinical differences between antisocial and primary alcoholics. *Comprehensive Psychiatry, 25: 1-8.*

City Collegiate. *Properties of Magnets.* Retrieved September 8, 2012, from http://www.citycollegiate.com/chapter17_Xc.htm

Clark, J. & Stoffel, V.C. (1992). Assessment of codependency behavior in two health student groups. *American Journal of Occupational Therapy, 46(9)*, 821-828.

Cleckley, H. (1982). *The Mask of Sanity (Mosby medical library)* (revised). Plume.

Cloud, J. (2009). The mystery of borderline personality disorder. *Time*. Retrieved from http://www.time.com/time/magazine/article/0,9171,1870491,00.html

Co-Dependents Anonymous (2010). *Patterns and characteristics of codependence*. Retrieved from http://coda.org/tools4recovery/patterns-new.htm

Coelho, P. (2006). *The Alchemist: A Fable about Following Your Dream* (A.R. Clarke, Trans.). Logan, IA: Perfection Learning. (Original work published in 1995)

Creswell, J. & Thomas Jr., L. (2009). The talented mr. Madoff. *New York Times*. Retrieved from http://www.nytimes.com/2009/01/25/business/25bernie.html

Crompton, S. (2008). *All about me: Loving a narcissist*. HarperCollins UK.

Derefinko, K. & Widiger, T. (2008). Antisocial personality disorder. In S.H. Fatemi et al (Ed.), *The medical basis of psychiatry* (3rd ed.). New York, NY: Humana Press.

DeWall, N.C., Pond Jr., R.S., Campbell, K.W., & Twenge, J.M. (2011) Tuning in to psychological change: Linguistic markers of psychological traits and emotions over time in popular U.S. song lyrics. *Psychology of Aesthetics, Creativity and the Arts*, 5(3), 200-207.

Dingfelder, S.F. (2011). Reflecting on narcissism: Are young people more self-obsessed than ever before? *American Psychological Association,Monitor on Psychology*, 42(2), 64.

Edelman, R. & Kupferberg, A. (2002). *Matthau: A life*. Lanham, MD: Taylor Trade Publishing.

Emilien, G., Durlach, C., Lepola, U., & Dinan, T. (2002). *Anxiety disorders: Pathophysiology and pharmacological treatment*. Boston, MA: Birkhäuser.

Everett, D. (2006). *Antisocial personality disorder vs. psychopathy: An analysis of the literature* (Thesis, Auburn University, 2006). Retrieved from http://etd.auburn.edu/etd/bitstream/handle/10415/360/EVERETT_DAVID_59.pdf

Farnsworth, R. & Edelman, R. (2010, December). *Jack Lemmon biography*. Retrieved from http://www.filmreference.com/ Actors- and-Actresses-Le-Ma/Lemmon-Jack.html

Fazel, S. & Danesh, J. (2002). Serious mental disorder in 23,000 prisoners: A systematic review of 62 surveys. *The Lancet*, 359: 545.

Flew, A. (Ed.) (1979). Golden rule. *A Dictionary of Philosophy*. London, UK: Pan Books.

Fraley, R.C. (2010). *A brief overview of adult attachment theory and research*. Retrieved from http://internal.psychology.illinois. edu/~rcfraley/attachment.htm

Freud, S. (1990). The psychogenesis of a case of homosexuality in a woman. In Strachey (Ed. & Trans.), *The standard edition of the complete psychological works of Sigmund Freud* (Vol. 18, pp. 145-172). London: Hogarth Press. (Original work published 1920)

Freud, S. (1963). Analysis terminable and interminable. In P. Rieff (Ed.), *Sigmund Freud: Therapy and technique* (pp. 233-271). New York: Collier. (Original work published 1937)

Frost, R. (1920). The Road Not Taken. *Mountain Interval*. New York, NY: Henry Holt.

Fuller, C. (2009, Oct 10). Therapist, heal thyself. Message posted to http://www.jung-at-heart.com/jung_at_heart/therapist_heal_ thyself.html

Goldberg, C. (1994). *On being a psychotherapist*. Northvale, NJ: Jason Aronson, Inc.

Grant, B. F., Chou, S. P., Goldstein, R. B., Huang, B., Stinson, F. S., Saha, T. D., et al. (2008). Prevalence, correlates, disability, and comorbidity of DSM-IV borderline personality disorder: Results from the Wave 2 National Epidemiologic Survey on Alcohol and Related Conditions. *Journal of Clinical Psychiatry*, 69(4), 533-45.

Hare, R.D. (1993). *Without conscience: The disturbing world of psychopaths among us*. New York, NY: Pocket Books.

Hare, R.D. (1996). Psychopathy and antisocial personality disorder: A case of diagnostic confusion. *Psychiatric Times*, 13(2).

Hare, R.D. (2003). *The Hare psychopathy checklist-revised (PCL-R)* (2nd ed.). Toronto, ON, Canada: Multi-Health Systems.

Hare, R.D. (2008). Psychopathy: A clinical construct whose time has come. *Current Perspectives in Forensic Psychology and Criminal Behavior* (2nd Ed.). Thousand Oaks, CA: Sage Publications.

Harlow, H.F. (1962). Development of affection in primates. In E.L. Bliss (Ed.), *Roots of behavior* (pp. 157-166). New York, NY: HarperCollins.

Harvard Mental Health Letter. (2006, January). Carl Rogers' client centered therapy: Under the microscope. Harvard University.

Hazan, C. & Shaver, P. (1987). Romantic love conceptualized as an attachment process. *Journal of Personality and Social Psychology*, 52(3), 511-524.

Helzer, J.E. & Przybeck, T.R. (1988). The co-occurrence of alcoholism with other psychiatric disorders in the general population and its impact on treatment. *Journal of Studies on Alcohol*, 49, 219–224.

Hotchkins, S. & Masterson, J. (2003). *Why is it always about you? The seven deadly sins of narcissism.* New York, NY: Free Press.

John, E. & Taupin, B. (1973, May). Candle in the Wind [Song]. *On Goodbye Yellow Brick Road.* Universal City, CA: MCA Records

Kassel, M. (2012). *The odd couple.* Retrieved from http://www.museum.tv/eotvsection.php?entrycode=oddcouplet

Kelley, D., & Kelley, T. (2006). *Alcoholic relationship survival guide: What to do when you don't know what to do.* Port Charlotte, FL: Kelley Training Systems, Inc.

Kerns, J. (2008, Sept. 15). Sociopath vs. psychopath: There is a difference. Posted to http://voices.yahoo.com/sociopath-vs-psychopath-there-difference-1906224.html

Kerr, M. & Bowen, M. (1988). *Family Evaluation.* New York, NY: W.W. Norton & Co.

Keys, D. (2012). Narcissists exposed - 75 things narcissists don't want you to know. Washington, DC: Light's House Publishing.

Kilpatrick, J. (1993). *Overused word of the 90's: "Dysfunctional."* Universal Press Syndicate.

Kreisman, J. & Straus, H. (2010). *I hate you--don't leave me: Understanding the borderline personality.* New York, NY: Perigree Trade.

Laign, J. (1989a). Co-dependency "has arrived." *Focus on the Family and Chemical Dependency* (November/December), 1-3.

Laign, J. (1989b). A patient poll. *Focus on the Family and Chemical Dependency* (pp. 16).Lasch, C. (1991). The culture of narcissism: American life in an age of diminishing expectations (Rev. ed.) New York, NY: W.W. Norton & Company.

Lennard, J. & Davis, L. (2008). *Obsession: A history.* Chicago, IL: University of Chicago Press.

Levy, K.N., Meehan, K.B., Kelly, K.M., Reynoso, J.S., Clarkin, J.F., & Kernberg, O.F. (2006). Change in attachment patterns and reflective function in a randomized control trial of transference-focused psychotherapy for borderline personality disorder. *Journal of Consulting and Clinical Psychology,* 74, 1027-1040.

Lewis, C.E., Rice, J., & Helzer, J.E. (1983). Diagnostic interactions: Alcoholism and antisocial personality. *Journal of Nervous and Mental Disease,* 171, 105–113.

Light's Blogs (2009). *The four dysfunctional family roles: The scapegoat.* Retrieved from http://lightshouse.org/lights-blog/the-four-dysfunctional-family-roles#axzz2IklrvlmF

Linehan, M. (1993). *Cognitive-behavioral treatment of borderline personality disorder.* New York, NY: The Guilford Press.

Loeterman, B. (Director/Producer). (2001). *American experience: Public enemy* #1 [Television movie]. Boston, MA: PBS Film WGBH. Retrieved from http://www.pbs.org/wgbh/amex/dillinger/peopleevents/p_frechette.html

Lydon, J. E., Jamieson, D. W., & Zanna, M. P. (1988). Interpersonal similarity and the social and intellectual dimensions of first impressions. *Social Cognition,* 6(4), 269-286.

Maccoby, M. (2004). *Narcissistic Leaders: The Incredible Pros, the Inevitable Cons.* Watertown, MA: Harvard Business Review.

Malmquist, C.A. (2006). *Homicide: A Psychiatric Perspective.*
Washington, DC: American Psychiatric Publishing, Inc.

Marsh, E. & Wolfe, D. (2008). *Abnormal Child Psychology* (4th ed.).
Independence, KY: Wadsworth Publishing.

Maslow, A. (1966). *The psychology of science: A reconnaissance.*
New York, NY: Harper & Row.

McBride, K. (2011). Narcissism and entitlement: Do I have to stand
in line? Posted to http://www.psychologytoday.com/blog/the-
legacy-distorted-love/201108/narcissism-and-entitlement-do-i-
have-stand-in-line

McGinnis, P. (2009). *Codependency-abandonment of self.* Retrieved
from http://www.dr-mcginnis.com/codependency.htm

Meloy, J.R. (2007). *Antisocial Personality Disorder.* Retrieved from
http://forensis.org/PDF/published/2007_AntisocialPerso.pdf

Codependency. (n.d.) Retrieved from http://www.merriam-webster.com/
dictionary/codependency

Michaels, S. (2013). Dickhead and Putz: Walter Matthau and Jack
Lemmon. Retrieved January 1, 2013 from http://www.findadeath.
com/Deceased/m/Matthau%20Lemmon/www.htm

Miller, A. (1979). *The drama of the gifted child: The search for the true
self.* New York, NY: Basic Books.

Miller, F. T., Abrams, T., Dulit, R., & Fyer, M. (1993). Substance abuse
in borderline personality disorder. *American Journal of Drug and
Alcohol Abuse*, 19, 491-497.

Moeller,G. & Dougherty, G. (2006). *Antisocial Personality Disorder,
Alcohol and Aggression.* Retrieved from http://pubs.niaaa.nih.
gov/publications/arh25-1/5-11.htm

Morrigan, D. (2012). *You're Not Crazy, It's Your Mother!* London, UK:
Darton Longman & Todd.

Morrigan, D. (2012). *Golden Child/Scapegoat.* Retrieved from http://
www.daughtersofnarcissisticmothers.com/golden-child-
scapegoat.html

Myers, I.B. (1980, 1995). Gifts Differing: Understanding Personality
Type. Mountain View, CA: CPP, Inc.

Norcross, J., Bike, D., & Evans, K. (2009). The therapist's therapist: A replication and extension 20 years later. *Psychotherapy: Theory, Research, Practice, Training*, 46: 32-41.

Nordqvist, C. (2012, February 24). *What is borderline personality disorder (BPD)?* Retrieved March 14, 2012 from http://www.medicalnewstoday.com/articles/9670.php

Nour, Al-Ali. (2012). Objects of co-dependency: Just between you and me. Retrieved from http://blog.nouralali.com/fromkeetra/

Oliver, D. (2004-2012). *Antisocial personality disorder (APD)*. Retrieved December 10, 2012 from http://www.bipolarcentral.com/otherillnesses/apd.php

Payson, E. (2002, 2009). *The wizard of oz and other narcissists*. Royal Oak, MI: Julian Day Publications.

Perry, S. (2003). *Loving in flow: How the happiest couples get and stay that way*. Napierville, IL: Sourcebooks, Inc.

Perskie, J. (2003, July 6). A wise & perceptive book that changed my life! [Review of the book *The Drama of the Gifted Child*]. Posted to http://www.amazon.com/review/R3M023OI4ID0AI/ref=cm_cr_dp_title?ie=UTF8&ASIN=0465012612&nodeID=283155&store=books

Pope, K. & Tabachnick, B. (1994). Therapists as patients: A national survey of psychologists' experiences, problems, and beliefs. *Professional Psychology: Research and Practice*, 25(3), 247-258.

Porr, V. (2001). How advocacy is bringing borderline personality disorder into the light: Advocacy issues. Retrieved December 4, 2012 from http://www.tara4bpd.org/ad.html

Prabhakar, K. (2006). *Proceedings of third AIMS international conference on management: An analytical study on assessing human competencies based on tests*. January 1-4, 2006. Ahmedabad: Indian Institute of Management.

Reik, T. (2011). *A psychologist looks at love*. NY: Ellott Press.

Robins, L. & Regier, D. (1990). *Psychiatric disorders in America: The epidemiologic catchment area study*. New York: Free Press.

Roe, A. (1964). Personality structure and occupational behavior. In H. Borow (Ed.), *Man in a world at work*. Boston: Houghton Mifflin.

Santoro, J., Tisbe, M., & Katsarakes,M. (1997). *An equifinality model of borderline personality disorder*. Retrieved from http://www.aaets.org/article20.htm

Schroeder, L. (2011). *The author*. Retrieved March 12, 2011 from http://evelynfrechette.com/author.html

Stapleton, C., (2009). *Melody Beattie Interview* in Palm Beach Post. Retrieved from http://www.palmbeachpost.com/accent/content/accent/epaper/2009/01/06/a1d_melody_web_0106.html

Lawrence, J. (2012). *Do opposites attract?* Retrieved December 4, 2012 from http://www.webmd.com/sex-relationships/features/do-opposites-attract

Sacramento County Local Child Care and Development Planning Council. (2000). *Proposal to Children and Family Commission*. Sacramento, CA: Author.

Stone, M. (1990). *The Fate of Borderline Patients: Successful Outcomes and Psychiatric Practice*. New York: The Guilford Press.

Straker, D. (2010). *Changing minds: In detail* (2nd Ed). Syque Press.

Swartz, M., Blazer, D., George, L., & Winfield, I. (1990). Estimating the prevalence of borderline personality disorder in the community. *Journal of Personality Disorders*, 4, 257-272.

Tennov, D. (1979, 1998). *Love and limerence: The experience of being in love* (1-2 Eds.). Chelsea, MI: Scarborough House.

Twenge, J. (2012). *Millennials: The greatest generation or the most narcissistic?* Retrieved June 1, 2012, from http://www.theatlantic.com/national/archive/2012/05/millennials-the-greatest-generation-or-the-most-narcissistic/256638

Twenge, J. (2010). *Generation me: Why today's young Americans are more confident, assertive, entitled--and more miserable than ever.* New York, NY: Free Press.

U.S. Department of Health and Human Services: Substance Abuse and Mental Health Services Administration. (2011). *Report to congress on borderline personality disorder*. HHS Publication No: SMA11-4644.

Walster, E.G., Walster, W., Berscheid, K., & Dion, K. (1971). Physical attractiveness and dating choice: A test of the matching hypothesis. *Journal of Experimental Social Psychology*, 7(2), 173.

Whitfield, C. (1984). Co-dependency An emerging problem among professionals. In J. Woititz, S. Wegscheider-Cruse, & C. Whitfield (Eds.), *Co-dependency: An emerging issue*. Deerfield Beach, FL: Health Communications.

What is the difference between a sociopath and a psychopath? Retrieved January 13, 2013 from WikiAnswers: http://wiki.answers.com

Whyte, D. (1997). *The house of belonging*. Langley, WA: Many Rivers Press.

Withrow, R. L. (2005). The use of metaphor in counseling couples. In G. R. Walz & R. K. Yep (Eds.), *VISTAS: Compelling perspectives on counseling* (pp. 119-122). Alexandria, VA: American Counseling Association.

World Health Organization. (1992). *ICD-10 classification of mental and behavioral disorders: Clinical descriptions and diagnostic guidelines*. Geneva, Switzerland: World Health Organization.

REFERENCE WEBSITES

http://www.mirrorhistory.com/mirror-history/history-of-mirrors/

http://allpsych.com/disorders/personality/antisocial.html

http://allpsych.com/disorders/personality/borderline.html

http://allpsych.com/disorders/personality/narcissism.html

http://www.madehow.com/Volume-1/Mirror.html#b

http://www.alanon.org.za/

http://bowencenter.org/

http://don-carter.com/

http://www.changingminds.org

http://www.slshealth.com

http://eresources.lib.unc.edu/external_db/external_database_auth.html

45640330R00110

Made in the USA
Middletown, DE
18 May 2019